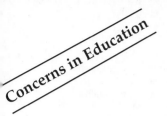

W9-APV-477

Bringing the District Back In: The Role of The Central Office in Instruction and Achievement

Martha Abele Mac Iver
Elizabeth Farley-Ripple

ERS

Because research and information make the difference.

Educational Research Service
1001 North Fairfax Street, Suite 500 • Alexandria, VA 22314-1587
Phone: 703-243-2100 • Toll Free: 800-791-9308
Fax: 703-243-1985 • Toll Free: 800-791-9309
Email: ers@ers.org • Web site: www.ers.org

Educational Research Service is the nonprofit organization serving the research and information needs of the nation's preK-12 education leaders and the public. Founded by the national school management associations, ERS provides quality, objective research and information that enable education leaders to make the most effective school decisions in both day-to-day operations and long-range planning. Refer to the end of this book for information on the benefits of an annual ERS subscription, and for an order form listing resources that complement this book. Or visit us online at www.ers.org for an overview of available resources.

ERS e-Knowledge Portal
http://portal.ers.org

ERS Founding Organizations:
American Association of School Administrators
American Association of School Personnel Administrators
Association of School Business Officials International
National Association of Elementary School Principals
National Association of Secondary School Principals
National School Public Relations Association

ERS Executive Staff:
Katherine A. Behrens, Acting President and Chief Operating Officer
Kathleen McLane, Chief Knowledge Officer

Library of Congress Cataloging-in-Publication Data
Mac Iver, Martha Abele.
Bringing the district back in : the role of the central office in instruction and achievement / Martha Abele Mac Iver, Elizabeth Farley-Ripple.
        p. cm.
Includes bibliographical references.
ISBN 978-1-931762-70-0
        1. School districts—United States. 2. School improvement programs—United States. 3. School management and organization—United States. I. Farley-Ripple, Elizabeth. II. Title.

LB2817.3.M33 2008
371.2'03—dc22   2007050525

Authors: Martha Abele Mac Iver and Elizabeth Farley-Ripple
Editor: Cheryl Bratten
Layout & Design: Joe Broderick and Libby McNulty

Ordering Information: Additional copies of this publication may be purchased at the base price of $28.00; ERS School District Subscriber: $14.00; ERS Individual Subscriber: $21.00). Quantity discounts available. Add the greater of $4.50 or 10% of total purchase price for shipping and handling. Phone orders accepted with Visa, MasterCard, or American Express. Stock No. 0712. ISBN 978-1-931762-70-0.

Table of Contents

Acknowledgements

The authors would especially like to thank Emily Williams for her research assistance. We also thank the following people who offered comments on earlier drafts of this report: Sam Stringfield, Deborah Land, Joseph Murphy, and Kenneth Leithwood. The authors also thank the Center for Research on the Education of Students Placed At Risk (CRESPAR), at Johns Hopkins University, which published an earlier version of this work in 2003.

Martha Abele Mac Iver
Elizabeth Farley-Ripple

About the Authors

 **Martha Abele Mac Iver** is Associate Research Scientist at the Center for Social Organization of Schools at Johns Hopkins University. She received her B.A. in European Studies at Michigan State University and her M.A. and Ph.D. in Political Science from the University of Michigan. She made the transition into educational policy research after more than a decade of research on the political transformation of Europe, and has a special interest in comparing the process of privatization in these two spheres. Dr. Mac Iver has written many reports and journal articles on European politics and the conflict in Northern Ireland, and has more recently published articles on such educational reform issues as vouchers, educational privatization, alternative certification, new teacher retention, high school reform, and other comprehensive school reform issues.

 **Elizabeth Farley-Ripple** is a doctoral student in Education Policy at the University of Pennsylvania Graduate School of Education. Her dissertation is a case study of evidence-based decision making at the school district level, focusing on curricular and instructional decisions in response to accountability policy. She received an M.A. in Quantitative Methods in the Social Sciences from Columbia and used those skills as a research assistant at the Center for Social Organization of Schools at Johns Hopkins University before beginning her doctoral studies. Her research covers a range of educational topics, including evidence-based decision making, teacher policy, predictors of student dropout and achievement, career and technical education, and alternative certification.

Chapter 1:

The District Context

Criticizing school district bureaucracies has become a growth industry over the past couple of decades. Horror stories of "mismanagement, waste, and corruption" from the infamous 110 Livingston Street (headquarters of the New York City public school system) abound: "Like a huge dinosaur, it is not particularly smart, has an insatiable appetite, moves awkwardly, yet exudes great power. Like wisteria, it is impossible to control; clip it back and it grows more vigorously than before. Like a giant octopus, its many tentacles reach fearlessly into every aspect of the school system" (Ravitch & Viteritti, 1997, p. 19). Crowson & Boyd (1992, p. 98) characterized the "internal politics of the organization of urban schooling … [as] remarkably adept at resisting adaptation, at serving the self-interests of school district personnel and at organizational maintenance above goal attainment." Or as J. A. Murphy (1994, p. 80) stated more bluntly, reflecting on his first days as Superintendent in Charlotte-Mecklenburg:

> The internal probe was straightforward. It confirmed my worse suspicions. Like so many other school districts, the administrative imperatives in Charlotte were all bureaucratic. Central

management had become slack, top-heavy, and ponderous. No one in the system was held to high standards—not students, not teachers, not administrators. To the contrary, self-protection and back scratching were the orders of the day...the organization had begun to serve itself—the employees—rather than its customers—students and parents.

A parent symbolized a large school system in this comment to researchers: "It's a mainframe school system in a PC world" (Jones & Hill, 1998, p. 141).

> *In the face of all this anti-district and anti-central office rhetoric, it is important to recognize the growing number of scholars who are emphasizing the importance of the district in school reform efforts and the research base that examines the role of the central office.*

Chubb and Moe (1990) linked higher student achievement to lower levels of bureaucratic organization in schools, setting off a veritable privatization revolution in education despite the methodological critiques of their analysis (e.g., Sukstorf, Wells, & Crain, 1993). Similarly, Peterson's (1999) analysis of National Education Longitudinal Study (NELS) data provided evidence that central district office power had a negative effect on student achievement, through its negative effect on school climate. Some observers have questioned the need for school districts at all. Finn (1991) claimed that "the

school is the vital delivery system, the state is the policy set-
ter (and chief paymaster), and nothing in between is very
important." Keedy (1994, p. 95) argued that "the pressures
for school decentralization are so intense that school sites
ultimately will replace districts as the administrative unit
in schooling." Others have proposed downsizing or dra-
matically scaled back functions for districts (Effron & Concannon, 1995; Hill, 1997; Parsley, 1991; Scambio & Graeber,
1991)[1] or large reductions in the administrator-to-student
ratio in large school districts (Ornstein, 1989). Restructuring, school-based management (SBM), and charter school
development have similarly become the cornerstones of
reform efforts for more than a decade, despite the mixed
evidence of effectiveness in improving student achievement
(e.g., Murphy & Beck, 1995; Murphy & Shiffman, 2002).

In the face of all this anti-district and anti-central office
rhetoric, it is important to recognize the growing number of
scholars who are emphasizing the importance of the district
in school reform efforts and the research base that examines
the role of the central office. Much of this work is necessarily
focused on larger, urban districts with larger central offices,
since more than half the school districts in the United States
have only a handful of central office employees (perhaps
only a superintendent and a business director) and many

---

[1] See Berg, Hall & Difford, 1996, however, for a study of the negative impact of
the downsizing process.

have no research and evaluation office (J. Murphy, personal communication, July 3, 2003). But the large majority of children in this country attend schools that are nested within district and state level organizations whose impact cannot be ignored. There is also growing evidence that schools need an effective intermediary in their relationships to the state.

This review of the role of school district central offices in improving instruction and raising student achievement builds on previous reviews of the role of school boards (Land, 2002) and superintendents (Thomas, 2002), where the focus was more on governance and leadership than on the particular activities undertaken by central office administrators. Though it is difficult in many cases to disentangle the role of the central office administration from its leader (the superintendent or CEO), our focus on the functional tasks of the central office addresses issues beyond the leadership role. We build and expand on earlier literature reviews on the district central office included in Elmore (1993), Hightower (2002), Lasky (2002), Marsh (2000), and Murphy (1994), by adding an analytical focus on the links between the central office and the process of improving instruction and student achievement. While acknowledging that the district central office is the product of a complex historical development (see Weeres, 1993) and is situated within a complex political environment influenced by numerous external actors (see Wong, 1992), we focus on the dynamics of relations between the central office and its schools (with their principals, teachers, and students). What contribution, if any, does the central office make to its schools to help improve classroom instruction and student achievement? How does recent research illuminate the connections between central office activity and the goal of schooling—student learning?

To select literature relevant to the relationship between school system central offices and student achievement in the United States, we began by conducting an ERIC database search using the keywords "central office and achievement," "district office and achievement," and "evaluation office." Our decision to focus on literature produced since 1978 was an attempt to make a comprehensive look at work over the past quarter century with a manageable task. This search yielded numerous studies only remotely related to student achievement. Based on analyses of these ERIC abstracts, we decided to exclude literature focused on school system functions such as food service, facilities, custodial services, transportation, and technical budgeting issues. Since the issue of SBM has already received considerable attention (e.g., Leithwood & Menzies, 1998; Mohrman & Wohlstetter, 1994; Murphy & Beck, 1995; see review in Land, 2002), we did not attempt to include all literature with that particular focus, though some articles concerned with discussing the role of the central office under SBM were relevant to our focus on instruction and achievement. We also excluded evaluations of particular programs or reform efforts that were only tangentially related to the central office.

Of particular interest for this review were publications or reports focused on the role of central office in:

- curriculum and instruction,
- professional development (both for teachers and principals),
- facilitating the implementation of specific reforms (either externally or internally developed) to improve instruction and student achievement, and
- research and evaluation related to student achievement.

Bibliographies from publications identified in the ERIC search provided an additional source of publications for the literature review, selected according to the same criteria described above.

The review proceeds by first analyzing studies (since the late 1970s) of the central office in more or less chronological order. We then examine the more recent studies by type of study, and then proceed to a more functional analysis of the roles of the central office with respect to improving instruction and student achievement. We conclude by outlining how the district, and in particular, central office activity, matters for student achievement, and kinds of research that still need to occur to further our understanding.

Chapter 2:

An Overview of Research on the District Central Office

L iterature focusing on the district central office can be generally categorized in four ways. Earlier research on the role of the district office in improving instruction and student achievement was built on the foundation of effective schools research (e.g., Brookover, Beady, Flood, Schweitzer, & Wisenbaker, 1979; Brookover & Schneider, 1975; Edmonds, 1979; Lezotte, Edmonds, & Ratner, 1974; Lezotte, Hathaway, Miller, Passalacqua, & Brookover, 1980). More recent research on district offices examines "positive outlier" districts in a state, or provides case studies of large urban school districts or comparative case studies of several districts from several states.

Effective Schools Research

Research on effective schools introduced the issue of the central office role in instructional improvement and student achievement, though critics noted the failure of this body of work to consider the district context (e.g., Cuban, 1984; Purkey & Smith, 1983). Researchers such as Wimpelberg (1987) pointed out candidly that despite the evidence of effective schools here and there, most teachers and principals do not exhibit the characteristics of those found in "effective schools" and there is a need for leadership at the district level to help assure that more individual schools become effective schools. Eubanks and Levine (1983), Crandall (1984), and Fullan (1985) argued from research findings that central office administrators are crucial in the school improvement process.

> "Depending on which school a child attends and to which classrooms the child is assigned, the student will encounter a varied array of programs and activities …. From the students' perspective, then, the quality of their educational experiences rests on the 'luck of the draw.' The central office instructional role is to remove this luck factor from the instructional program, i.e., to insure that idiosyncratic variations in programs, people, and policies do not result in systematic differences in the quality of education for children" (Corbett & Wilson, 1992, p. 46).

The proliferation of research and discussion about "effective schools" spawned a National Center for Effective Schools Research and Development (NCESRD) at Michigan

State University and the University of Wisconsin-Madison during the 1980s and early 1990s, as well as an "Effective Schools Process" national training program that influenced numerous school districts throughout the country (see Bullard & Taylor, 1993, for a selected list of districts with successful implementation). The effective schools principles, with their emphasis on instructional leadership by the principal, coincided well with a growing emphasis on SBM. However, the theme of what districts could do—and needed to do—to help schools become effective schools became more prominent through various case studies of districts that had adopted the process (Bullard & Taylor, 1993; Hall, Putnam, & Hord, 1985; Meyers and Sudlow, 1992; Middleton, Smith, & Williams, 1994; Stoll & Fink, 1992). These studies emphasized the importance of the superintendent's leadership, the transformation of central office culture to be more flexible and service-oriented than regulatory and monitor-oriented, and the role of districtwide staff development at all levels. As one of the district case studies in Bullard and Taylor (1993) illustrates, useful central office support includes technical assistance in areas such as the following: monitoring academic progress, following a curriculum review and development cycle, establishing a positive school climate, providing staff development that addresses teacher expectations for student achievement, and creating structures that will develop new administrative leaders for the district. The research quality of studies varied widely, from the primarily journalistic approach of Bullard and Taylor (1993) to the more rigorous longitudinal study of implementation and outcomes (including comparison district outcomes) of Meyers and Sudlow (1992).

Several other externally developed models of district level reform also surfaced in our literature search. The Achievement-Directed Leadership (ADL) program (Biester, 1983, 1984; French, 1984; Graeber et al., 1984; Helms & Heller, 1985; Helms et al., 1985; Larkin, 1984), developed by the Philadelphia-based organization, Research for Better Schools (RBS), had evidence of student achievement gains in reading and mathematics directly correlated with the level of program implementation. The program involved training for central office personnel first in how to implement research-based practices for effective instruction and monitoring progress, followed by training for principals and then for teachers. Though ADL does not appear to have continued past 1985 as a research-based intervention, its principles appear to have survived in the RBS school improvement consultations and its tools for district leaders (Beyer & Houston, 1988; Buttram, Corcoran, & Hansen, 1989; Dusewicz & Beyer, 1991; McGrail, Wilson, Buttram, & Rossman, 1991; Wilson, 1985; Wilson & McGrail, 1987).

The Onward to Excellence program developed by the Northwest Regional Laboratory (NWREL) involved training district and school staff in a "10-step process designed to become a tool for cyclical school improvement" (Blum & Butler,

---

Onward to Excellence 10-Step Process for Cyclical School Improvement

1. Organize for improvement
2. Study the research base and findings
3. Profile student performance
4. Set a goal for improvement
5. Check current instructional practice
6. Develop a research-based prescription for improvement
7. Prepare for implementation
8. Implement the prescription
9. Monitor implementation
10. Evaluate progress and renew efforts

(Northwest Regional Educational Laboratory, Blum & Butler, 1987).

1987, p. 7). Other "models" were found in books of advice for district leaders regarding how the central office could be organized and mobilized for monitoring progress, planning improvement, and implementing action to improve student achievement (e.g., Genck, 1983; Klausmeier, 1985; Leithwood, Aitken, & Jantzi, 2001; Mauriel, 1989), and were often based on the authors' consulting experience with school districts.

Apart from specific district level interventions, such as the ADL program described above, studies conducted before the 1990s found little attention at the district office level to curriculum and instruction issues, or equipping school principals to lead effectively in this area (Crowson & Morris, 1985; Floden et al., 1984; Floden et al., 1988; Hannaway & Sproull, 1978-79; Rowan, 1982). As Elmore (1993) summarized this literature, there was a tendency for "key decisions on curriculum and teaching [to be] passed from states to districts, from districts to principals, and from principals to teachers, with little effective focus or guidance" (p. 116). In a later analysis, Elmore (2000) situated the lack of attention by most central office administrators to the instructional or technical "core" within the theory of loose coupling (Meyer & Rowan, 1992; Weick, 1976). As Elmore (2000, p. 6) summarized it:

> The administrative superstructure of the organization—principals, board members, and administrators—exists to "buffer" the weak technical core of teaching from outside inspection, interference, or disruption. Administration in education, then, has come to mean not the management of instruction but the management of the structures and processes around instruction.

Some early studies of districts sought to identify district level and central office characteristics that could explain systemic improvement or higher-than-expected student achievement (Murphy & Hallinger, 1988; Pajak & Glickman, 1989) or at least the focus on instructional improvement that had attracted regional attention (Corbett & Wilson, 1991). Studies of successful or effective schools (e.g., Corcoran & Wilson, 1986) yielded findings about the role of the central office in contributing to their success (Miller, Smey-Richman, & Woods-Houston, 1987). Common themes emerged from these studies, including the importance of a focused message from the central office about the importance of student achievement and its relationship to quality instruction. Effective districts followed through on this focused message by providing time for staff to interact with each other about instruction, to receive professional development, and for experienced personnel to facilitate learning about improving instruction.

Other case studies of particular districts (Fitzgerald, 1993; Shipengrover & Conway, 1996) also emphasized the role of central office staff in providing professional development for teachers and focusing everyone on instruction and student learning. The national study of school-based reform conducted by Quellmalz, Shields, and Knapp (1995) included surveys of staff in more than 1,500 districts. It echoed previous conclusions and contributed additional advice about what district offices could do to support school-based reforms: provide professional development opportunities, find an appropriate balance between setting and waiving particular requirements, manage forces and conditions outside the school's control (teachers' unions, state requirements), and help schools to obtain additional resources. One drawback to these studies was the absence of qualitative data from comparison districts where student achievement was not higher than average or had not improved over time. Though their findings were intuitively reasonable, it was not possible to make causal conclusions attributing higher student achievement to these district-level factors.

Positive Outlier District Studies

Murphy and Hallinger (1988) were among the first to identify a group of high-performing districts and their distinguishing characteristics. Their study of 12 "instructionally effective" school districts in California noted an established instructional and curricular focus, consistency and coordination of instructional activities, strong instructional leadership from the superintendent, and an emphasis on monitoring instruction and curriculum. At the level of "organizational dynamics," these districts exhibited 1) rationality without bureaucracy, 2) structured district control with school autonomy, 3) a systems perspective with a "people orientation," and 4) strong leadership with an active administrative team (collaboration with strong leadership).

More recent studies of districts identified as high-performing, relative to the poverty level of their students, have been conducted in Texas (Ragland, Asera, & Johnson, 1999; Skrla, Scheurich, & Johnson, 2000) and North Carolina (Public Schools of North Carolina, 2000). The common themes emerging from these studies about central office practices observed in relatively high-performing or improving districts echoed those of Murphy and Hallinger (1998). They included:

- a climate of urgency regarding achievement improvement for all students;
- a sense that achievement was the primary responsibility of every staff member in the district;
- a shared sense of the central office as a support and service organization for the schools;
- a primary focus on improving instruction, accompanied by a high level of resources devoted to coherent professional development support linked to research-based practices;
- focused attention on analysis and alignment of curriculum, instructional practice and assessment; and
- professional development for principals in interpreting data to make good instructional decisions.

A study by Education Commission of the States researchers (Armstrong & Anthes, 2001) examined six districts in five states that had used data to improve student achievement. They found in each district office a "service orientation" culture focused on supporting principals and teachers to use student data for continuous improvement, combined with structural mechanisms for training and assessments. Cawelti and Protheroe's (2001) study of six high-poverty districts (Sacramento, Houston, two other smaller districts from Texas, one from Idaho, and one from West Virginia) all with systemwide (or notable, in the case of the larger urban districts) improvements in student achievement, found a similar focus on equipping teachers to use research-based

Characteristics of High-Performing Districts

- *Rationality without bureaucracy:* These systems had a clear purpose, a sense that the curriculum and instructional approaches emphasized could promote student learning, and patterns of outcome inspection and accountability. At the same time, there was little evidence of bureaucratic rigidity which often accompanies rational systems.

- *Structured district control with school autonomy:* There was a substantial amount of district-level direction in these school systems, including coordination and control over school-level activities and forced consistency between schools in these districts. However, this control was most noticeable when decisions were made and outcomes were inspected. Greater autonomy for schools was evident in the input and implementation stages of the decision process.

- *Systems perspective with people orientation:* It was evident that the achievement of district and school goals and the maintenance of organization systems were the major concerns of superintendents of these districts. Yet within this framework of purpose and expectations, there was evidence that staff needs were recognized and attended to.

- *Strong leadership with active administrative team:* The superintendents in these districts were generally powerful chief executive officers that did not shy away from making decisions or resolving problems. On the other hand, they consciously culled and used the expertise of their administrative staff.

(adapted from Murphy & Hallinger, 1988, pp. 178-179).

instructional practices and aligning curriculum with test content, as well as decentralizing management and budgeting to the school level.

The most comprehensive outlier study thus far, undertaken by MDRC for the Council of Great City Schools (Snipes, Doolittle, & Herlihy, 2002), involved retrospective case studies of three districts (Sacramento, Houston, and Charlotte-Mecklenberg) and a fourth "district within a district" (the New York City Chancellor's district). Each of these urban districts had been identified as showing consistent student achievement gains (at higher levels than their respective states) for at least 3 years and a narrowing of the achievement gap between white and minority students. Methodologically stronger than previous studies, this one included comparison districts in which student achievement had not similarly improved. Conclusions drawn by the authors from this exploratory study included the importance of: 1) a shared focus among school board, superintendent, and community leaders on student achievement as the primary goal, as well as a common vision about how to improve it; 2) developing instructional coherence through provision of standards, instructional frameworks, and intensive professional development to principals and teachers; and 3) equipping school level personnel for data-driven decision making. Snipes et al. argue that it is the combination of these components (rather than any one in isolation) that has made these districts effective in raising student achievement.

District Case Studies

Recent case studies of district-level initiatives in major urban school systems to improve instruction and student achievement have focused primarily on Philadelphia, New York's District #2, and San Diego. While the Chicago reforms have received much attention (e.g., Bryk, Sebring, Kerbrow, Rollow, & Easton, 1998; and numerous studies conducted by the Consortium on Chicago School Reform), there has been little focus on the role of the district or central office per se in improving instruction and student achievement. As Quinn, Stewart, and Nowakowski (1993) noted in their evaluation of systemwide school reform in Chicago, "There is little indication across the case sites that student achievement is the primary target of this reform ... Chicago school reform is primarily about governance and structure, not about curriculum and instruction" (p. 5). Bryk et al. (1998) concluded that the central office provided little assistance to Chicago schools, and that the lack of district infrastructure for capacity building at the school level helped to explain why the reforms were not particularly successful. Similarly, the Bay Area School Reform Collaborative (BASRC), an Annenberg-funded initiative, includes clusters of schools within districts, but has only recently begun to focus on districts. Its associated evaluation reports do not yet contribute to the literature on district-level efforts, except to note the willingness of districts like the San Bruno Park Elementary Schools District to adopt the BASRC "Cycle of Inquiry" reform process districtwide (Bay Area School Reform Collaborative, 2001, p. 11).

Philadelphia, the only whole district to receive funding from the Annenberg Challenge (for the Children Achieving initiative), was studied intensively by scholars from the Consortium for Policy Research in Education (CPRE). Their work yielded a report focused specifically on the role of the central office in pursuing instructional reform and improved student achievement (Foley, 2001), as well as other reports that touched on district-level variables and the role of central office personnel (e.g., Christman, 2001; Spiri, 2001). Foley (2001) uncovered significant desires of principals and school-based staff for more district support in selecting and implementing instructional programs that would help raise student achievement, a situation that conflicted with the reform initiative's intentions of promoting decentralized, school-level decision making. At the same time, some principals also voiced frustration over too much control by cluster leaders and too little freedom to pursue their own ideas (Spiri, 2001).

Studies of district-level reform efforts in New York's District #2 have focused on professional development for principals in instructional leadership (Elmore & Burney, 2000; Fink & Resnick, 1999), teacher professional development (Harwell, D'Amico, Stein, & Gatti, 2000; Resnick & Glennan, 2001), and content-specific principles of instruction (D'Amico, van den Heuvel, & Harwell, 2000; Stein & D'Amico, 1999; Stein,

Harwell, & D'Amico, 1999)—categories of district-level involvement which we analyze more fully later in this review. Studies of a similar reform effort in San Diego (Darling-Hammond, Hightower, Husbands, LaFors, & Young, 2002; Hightower, 2002), also spearheaded by Anthony Alvarado (leader of District #2 during the reforms discussed above), echo many of these themes. The Learning Research and Development Center at the University of Pittsburgh, which has hosted the High Performance Learning Communities (HPLC) project analyzing District #2, also hosts the Institute for Learning (IFL) program that is currently using the same district-level instructional principles in working with nine other urban districts,[1] though reports are not yet available on them.

Evidence of a link between these district office initiatives and improved student achievement is only tentative. Elmore and Burney (1997) noted that District #2 was 16th of 32 New York City districts in 1987 when Alvarado became superintendent, where one would expect it to be demographically, but in the latter years of the improvement strategy, it had advanced to become second. According to the HPLC (2000), between 1988 and 1998 the number of students performing at grade level in reading rose from 56% to 73% and in mathematics from 66% to 82%. D'Amico, Harwell, Stein, and van den Heuvel (2001) also sought to link district efforts to implement instructional improvement

---

[1] As listed in Resnick & Glennan (2001), these are Austin TX, Bridgeport CT, Columbia SC, Los Angeles CA, Kansas City MO, Pittsburgh PA, Providence RI, St. Paul MN, and Springfield MA.

to student achievement, but their study covered just one year. They presented evidence that achievement is higher in classrooms where teachers report having received high quality professional development in mathematics and claim to be using the Balanced Literacy approach (compared to other classrooms).

But there are obvious limitations to a cross-sectional study using teacher perceptions as the primary independent variable. Similarly, Resnick and Harwell (2000) found mixed evidence from analysis of cross-sectional data regarding the relationship between District #2 model variables and student achievement, based on regression and path analysis using school-level achievement and school-level rating scores on model components. Though there was a significant relationship between quality of teaching and student achievement, the study failed to find evidence of the more salient model's intervention variables of professional development and principal leadership. Harwell, D'Amico, Stein, and Gatti (2000) also failed to find a relationship between teachers' exposure to professional development and any reduction in the achievement gap in District #2, though it is unclear how representative the teacher sample was, given the low return rate of teacher surveys (12%). Darling-Hammond et al. (2002) documented improved student achievement in San Diego in aggregate levels over time, but more detailed analyses have yet to be completed in that district. Studies of Philadelphia's Children Achieving initiative found modest gains in student achievement, particularly at schools with stronger implementation of the reforms (school leadership focused on instruction, professional community among teachers, curriculum-based professional development, and effective use of data) (Christman, 2001; Corcoran & Christman, 2002; Tighe, Wang, & Foley, 2002). The initiative ended in 2000, however, and gains were not sufficient to prevent the state decision to pursue a privatization strategy (Gewertz, 2002).

Comparative District Studies

Comparative studies of district central offices, which are essential to further our understanding of their impact on student achievement, remain relatively few. The Smith and Mickelson (2000) study comparing student achievement outcomes in Charlotte-Mecklenburg Schools (CMS) with those in two other urban North Carolina districts concluded that the much acclaimed reforms in Charlotte (Doyle & Pimental, 1993; Murphy, 1995) had not resulted in that school system outperforming similar districts in the state (except in AP and higher level courses), but see Snipes, Doolittle, & Herlihy (2002) for evidence of positive effects in later years. Though the reforms focused the attention of all district personnel on accountability standards and student achievement, they involved significant cuts in central office staff and relied on a school-based management philosophy rather than on school capacity building by central office personnel.

The study suggests that accountability and standards-based reforms may be necessary but not sufficient for achieving significant achievement outcomes.

A comparative study of three unnamed urban districts (Corcoran, Fuhrman, & Belcher, 2001) explored the "role of central office staff members in shaping and supporting instructional reforms" (p. 79), and identified factors that constrained the effectiveness of central offices. At the "design and adoption" phase of the reform process, these central offices (like Philadelphia in the Foley, 2001, study) wrestled with how much they should prescribe reform practices to schools and how much freedom they should allow. One district was tempted by the funding to promote a strategy that no one really believed would be effective. As Corcoran et al. (2001, p. 80) summarized: "The emergence of evidence-based decision-making was hampered by whims, fads, opportunism, and ideology." In the "coordination and support of reform" phase, where the focus was on professional development, the districts were pulled in several directions simultaneously and did not demonstrate a commitment to measuring the effectiveness of professional development on teacher practice and student learning. The CPRE researchers noted that the districts were under pressure to achieve results quickly and scale up practices before the evidence was in on their effectiveness, and that changeover in the superintendency exacerbated the situation.

In reporting on findings from a larger CPRE study of 22 districts in 8 states over 2 years, Massell (2000, p. 1) emphasized that districts are increasingly giving attention to: 1) interpreting and using data, 2) building teacher knowledge and skill, 3) aligning curriculum and instruction, and 4) targeting interventions on low-performing students and/or schools. Arguing that the district office role is crucial for building a school's capacity in all these areas, Massell (2001) identified challenges that districts face. These included helping schools understand how to improve their student achievement data to determine classroom instruction, and equipping teachers to accomplish this. But this analysis did not address the relative effectiveness of different central office strategies in improving student achievement. Goertz's (2001) analysis, based on the same large study, focused on how differences in state accountability systems influence the district role. Districts in states with more high-stakes accountability systems had a structure that helped them to focus on student achievement, but this did not guarantee changes in classroom instructional practices. Districts' needs for resources (particularly human resources) to build capacity among principals and teachers emerged as a crucial issue from this study.

Other ongoing projects and studies involving multiple districts have not yet produced research reports. The Annenberg Institute for School Reform's "National Task Force on the Future of Urban Districts" (School Communities that Work) project is completing design proposals and intends to work "directly with several partner districts and organizations to test, implement, and evaluate new designs and practices" (Annenberg Institute, 2002). The Cross City Campaign for Urban School Reform, a national network of school reform leaders from Baltimore, Chicago, Denver, Houston, Los Angeles, New York, Oakland, Philadelphia and Seattle (Cross City Campaign, 2002), is engaged in a "multiyear research project to examine how district policies help or hinder school improvement in Chicago, Milwaukee, and Seattle" (Johnston, 2001, p. 19). Thus far it has produced only a prescriptive primer on "Reinventing Central Office" (Berne et al., 1995) and no research-based reports on the impact of central office activity on improved instruction and achievement outcomes.

Groups such as the National Commission on Teaching and America's Future (2002) have compiled resources for districts, such as a District Policy Inventory that are practice-oriented rather than research-oriented. There are district networks connected to other reform efforts, such as the Center for Leadership on School Reform (the Schlechty Group), but no comparative district research studies have emerged from these projects.

Chapter Summary: About the Research

In this chapter, we have found that among the vast literature addressing the role of central offices, most work is either mainly descriptive or prescriptive, and based on personal experience of the authors. Furthermore, many of the available research studies tend to focus narrowly on such issues as time use by central office administrators, surveys of what school-based personnel want from the central office, or central office administrators' perspectives on particular reform initiatives.

The most useful recent research studies tend to fall into three categories: district outlier studies, district case studies, and comparative district studies. There are particular methodological problems with drawing conclusions from most of these studies:

- District outlier studies have summarized characteristics of high-performing districts, but generally have not made comparisons with central office activity in lower-performing districts (recent work by Snipes, Doolittle, & Herlihy, 2002, is a welcome shift in this direction).
- District case studies may have longitudinal data over time, but generally have not included data from comparison districts.
- Comparative district studies have generally not examined student achievement outcomes.

Nonetheless, in our search we revealed a number of studies that go beyond description and prescription and deepen our understanding of the role of the central office in improving instruction and student achievement. In Chapter 3 we present these findings and discuss them in terms of three broad functions of the school district.

Challenges for Policy Makers and Practitioners in Building School Capacity

- **Comprehensiveness of Professional Development.** Administrators see a need to make the feedback loop between data and practice more explicit. Because teacher education programs do not show teachers how to use data to direct improvements to curriculum and instruction, professional development for teachers that targets the diagnostic uses of data are needed.

- **Complexity of Data.** Assessments generated by states, districts, schools and teachers result in an overwhelming amount of information to which teachers and administrators are expected to respond, and using these data amounts to a major intellectual challenge. Efforts are needed to help local educators make appropriate decisions based on multiple sources of information.

- **Tailoring Data Interpretations to Specific School Needs.** Many factors influence whether importing strategies of successful schools will have the same outcomes for another school. Helping educators to understand these differences is essential if adopting external practices is to be productive.

- **The Effects of Data on Focus.** Using data to drive decisions can result in frequent, quick shifts in policy focus as districts try to address the problems that data uncover from year to year. Thus policy makers and practitioners face the challenge of balancing the need for continuity in order to allow changes to take effect as well as the need for a feedback loop that allows for adjustments if success is not reached.

(adapted from Massell, 2001, p. 165-167)

Chapter 3

The Roles of the Central Office in Improving Instruction and Achievement

I n the previous chapter, we laid out some of the major studies conducted on the role of the district central office. The purpose of this chapter is to synthesize the existing body of literature in order to draw from it specific conclusions regarding the role of central office in improving instruction and student achievement.

The following sections examine various dimensions of the central office role relevant to the kind of instruction that will yield improvement in student achievement. Building on the framework outlined by Corcoran et al. (2001), we divide the central office role into several components:

- decision making about curriculum/instruction, with a section analyzing research on the role of the central

office in selecting and implementing externally developed reform models,

- supporting good instructional practice through professional development (for principals and teachers) and
other administrative supports, and

- evaluating results (including the role of the research and
evaluation office) and the feedback loop from evaluation to decision making and supporting instructional
practice (including scaling–up good practices).

Additionally, we build on the theoretical framework of
Spillane and Thompson (1997, p. 199), who measure district
capacity for reform by the dimensions of "human capital
(knowledge, skills, and dispositions of leaders within the
district), social capital (social links within and outside of the
district, together with the norms and trust to support open
communication via these links), and financial resources (as
allocated to staffing, time, and materials)."

Decision Making About Curriculum/Instruction

As Corcoran et al. (2001, p. 79) noted, the first task in instructional improvement is "deciding what to do." The
motto in an era of restructuring and school-based management is to leave this decision to the schools themselves.
Those advocating this position assume, either consciously or unconsciously, a relatively high level of human and
social capital at the school level—that the school has an

We construed the LEAs' capacity to support ambitious instructional reform primarily as a capacity to learn the substantive ideas at the heart of the new reforms and to help teachers and others within the district learn these ideas...In this view, learning is the process through which human capital is developed, and learning, or the development of human capital, depends critically on the development and exploitation of social capital. Some threshold value of financial resources is undoubtedly necessary as well, but the value of financial resources in the capacity building process is heavily conditioned by the levels of human and social capital in the district.

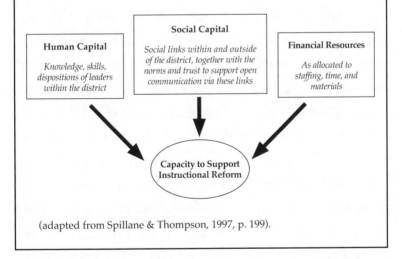

(adapted from Spillane & Thompson, 1997, p. 199).

instructional leader who knows what curriculum will best ensure student learning and high achievement, and a collegial staff who can deliver quality instruction and promote high levels of learning. While many fine examples of such schools exist, they generally do not constitute a majority, especially in large cities with high levels of poverty.

> *The first task in instructional improvement is "deciding what to do."*

Standards as a Complicating Factor

In the current policy context dominated by the themes of accountability and performance standards, educational leaders are increasingly aware of the need for decision making about curriculum and instruction to be linked to standards. Various studies have also shown that schools and their teachers need the district central office to help articulate and interpret state frameworks and/or student performance standards and to help teachers to know what to do in the classroom so that students will be able to meet those standards (Foley, 2001; Steineger & Sherman, 2001). Central office staff members have participated with other district personnel in developing academic standards for Chicago (Barth, 1994) and Philadelphia (Simon, Foley, & Passantino, 1998). Firestone, Rosenblum, and Webb (1987) pointed out how state policy contexts—such as the existence of a minimum competency test for graduation that is the main state accountability measure—can discourage urban districts from setting content standards for high school courses, a practice they found in other large urban districts not constrained by a minimalist state test. Fairman and Firestone (2001) linked differences in how district central offices build school level capacity for understanding state standards and teaching effectively for state assessments to both state policy contexts (degree of high stakes accountability) and beliefs and orientations of district leaders.

Districts such as Philadelphia that have sought to promote decentralized decision making about curriculum have found the need to become more prescriptive as school leaders demonstrate their need for guidance in selecting appropriate curriculum for standards-based instruction (Foley, 2001; Simon, Foley, & Passantino, 1998). As these authors pointed out, Philadelphia teachers needed more concrete help with unit and lesson planning to address the vague standards developed under the Children Achieving initiative. Decentralization efforts in Riverside, California, resulted in too much fragmentation in curriculum and instruction, leading that district to specify a scope and sequence and research-based instructional techniques (Berry, 1985). Grossman, Thompson, and Valencia (2001) noted the particular difficulties encountered by new teachers who receive only a set of performance standards with no other guidance from the school or central office on how to structure instruction to meet those goals. CPRE's longitudinal study of accountability systems in districts and schools in 10 states identified roles for the district office in helping schools to meet state standards, including guidance to principals and teachers in standards-based instruction and curricular frameworks (Goertz, 2001; Massell, 2000). Unfortunately, as evidenced by Corcoran et al. (2001), central offices often become bogged down by ideological or local political constraints and fail to provide the kind of curriculum and instruction guidance needed by the schools they serve.

Adoption of Externally Developed Programs

Districts are faced with choices among internally developed curriculum and instruction designs and externally developed reform models (many with their own defined curricula and instructional models). This is particularly true now in the current political climate that promotes evidence-based instructional practices and provides resources (through the Obey-Porter Comprehensive School Reform Demonstration Act) for schools and districts to adopt proven whole-school reform designs. Even though many reform models do not specify particular curricula, the process of adopting a reform model fits into the general category of "deciding what to do."[1] In studies of districts that encouraged and even mandated schools to select a research-based whole-school reform model (Datnow, Hubbard, & Meehan, 2002; Datnow

---

[1] To avoid unnecessary repetition, this discussion of the district role vis-à-vis externally developed reform models touches also on the theme discussed in the next section, supporting good instructional practice.

& Stringfield, 2000; Ross, 2001; Yonezawa & Stringfield, 2000), it was found that district office support was important through all stages of the implementation process: dissemination of information about models; helping schools to select models that are appropriate for their situation; and provision of ongoing support, including waiving conflicting requirements, as models are implemented in the schools. Datnow and Stringfield (2000) found a direct relationship between the level of district support and the level of reform model implementation in the schools. Ross (2001) stressed the difficulties involved in a district supporting too many different whole-school reform models a finding echoed by Corcoran et al., 2001, with respect to various district initiatives. Ross also pointed out problems with requiring either very high-achieving or very low-achieving schools to implement an externally developed model. The high-achieving schools do not need to do so, and will probably resent it, while the low-achieving schools probably do not have the capacity, without considerable intervention from the central office, to begin implementing such a model. Several studies (Datnow and Stringfield, 2000; Stringfield et al., 1999; Ross, 2001) highlighted the problems resulting from changes in district leadership, resulting in reduced support from the central office for implementation of the externally developed reform models. Studies of the New American Schools (NAS) implementation and performance (Berends, Kirby, Naftel, & McKelvey, 2001; Bodilly, 1998; Bodilly & Berends, 1999) also noted the importance of stable leadership, flexibility, and support in resource allocation from the district central office in sustaining implementation of the NAS models at schools. Echoing many of these findings, Murphy and Datnow (2003) also pointed out that critical roles of the central office include "helping schools see how school-level change efforts nest within the district's goals and the state's reform agenda" (p. 402) and assuring stability of school-level leadership.

Reform model developers and advocates have a particular perspective on the role of the district office in supporting externally developed reform model implementation. Mac Iver and Balfanz (2000) analyzed the role of the district office from their perspective as developers of Talent Development Middle Schools. Critiquing the contemporary commitment to site-based management among so many educational reformers, they argued that urban schools, like small businesses, are as likely to fail as to succeed due to lack of resources (especially human resources), lack of technical knowledge about effective curriculum and instruction, and unstable operating environments (teacher and principal mobility). There is a critical role for the school district central office in building an infrastructure that provides:

- continual professional development,
- in-class implementation support for reform models,
- organizational assistance (building effective school organizational structures, like small learning communities; providing budget information early, minimizing last-minute policy and staffing changes; adequate time for teachers to work collaboratively), and

- productive use of data (particularly student achievement data).

Without cooperation from the school district on these issues, even assistance from external partners and model development teams in these areas may be undermined.

Reflecting on the role of the district office in supporting Success for All (SFA), Slavin and Madden (1999) reported that districts seem to be more effective in sustaining a liaison function (though a district SFA coordinator) than providing for training and implementation monitoring with schools. School districts have often marginalized reform initiatives, such as SFA, by assigning them to low ranking central office personnel who may already have numerous other responsibilities and no experience in SFA schools. The SFA developers envision future recruitment of SFA principals for central office coordinator positions, so that they will be able to function more effectively in providing training and follow-up to schools. In a study of SFA in three California districts and one district in a southeastern state, Datnow and Castellano (2003) found that district level support for SFA was critical, but depended to a large extent on how well SFA schools were raising student test scores in the high-stakes accountability context in which the districts operated. If scores did not rise sufficiently, district support for SFA declined.

Studies of the role of the central office in supporting the Accelerated Schools model (Davidson, 1993; Finnan & Meza, 2003; Kuo, 1998) found that district office support could be helpful but was not necessary for schools to improve. District office support "can help foster accelerated schools process" (Davidson, 1993, p. 24) through:

- facilitating school level buy-in of restructuring,
- supporting the development of site-based decision making,
- providing professional development,
- revising evaluation procedures, and
- creating organizational structures to support Accelerated Schools (Kuo, 1998).

Echoing themes uncovered in earlier district office studies, central office staff in the three suburban districts supportive of Accelerated Schools in the Kuo (1998) study viewed their roles as "keeper of the mission/vision," "promoter of risk-taking and entrepreneurial activity," "capacity builder," and "service provider." Kirby and Meza (1995) summarized the developers' expectations of the district office in supporting the coaching model for training teachers in Accelerated Schools: recommending coach candidates, providing release time to coaches, nurturing schools involved in the Accelerated Schools process, and communicating to district stakeholders about the Accelerated Schools process. In their study of Accelerated Schools in Memphis, Finnan and Meza (2003) noted how district leadership change may have eliminated official support for Accelerated Schools as a comprehensive reform design, but those schools that had chosen it willingly and internalized the principles of the reform model continued to demonstrate characteristics of Accelerated Schools.

Echoing themes articulated by others, studies of the Coalition of Essential Schools (CES) (Cushman, 1991; Hall & Placier, 2003) pointed out the importance of district flexibility in school-based management. However, a district-supported professional development center in Louisville that emphasized CES principles was an important component of district support for the reform (Cushman, 1991). A study of the Modern Red Schoolhouse reform (Kilgore & Jones, 2003) noted a lack of support from the central office in demonstrating familiarity with the reform design and providing material resources, issues that were detrimental to implementation. Studies of Exemplary Center for Reading Instruction (ECRI) (Huberman, 1981; Huberman & Crandall, 1983), Achievement Via Individual Determination (AVID) (Hubbard & Mehan, 1999), and other reforms (Crandall, 1984; Crandall & Eiseman, 1983; Loucks & Cox, 1982) also emphasized the importance of central office support, especially in assuring that resources are available for professional development. Studies of Core Knowledge (Datnow, Borman, & Stringfield, 2000; Mac Iver, McHugh, & Stringfield, 2000) emphasized the need for districts to provide resources (especially teacher planning time) and pointed out how districts were influenced by state accountability systems to put pressure on Core Knowledge schools to devote more time to activities linked to test preparation, thus undermining implementation. Mac Iver's (2003) study of Direct Instruction (combined with Core Knowledge) in Baltimore indicated that districts could indeed institutionalize reforms within their central office structure, though the reform developer and others involved in implementation identified disadvantages as well as advantages to such structured district "support." Though the district office may offer formal support for the reform, it may also guide schools' decision making differently than the reform developer would advise, and hinder implementation by imposing uniform requirements across schools that the reform developer would not support (Berkeley, 2002).

Resource manuals for district leaders have now been developed by federally funded regional laboratories and other organizations. The manuals are designed to help district administrators through the process of assisting schools to consider, select, implement, and evaluate the effects of a reform model (e.g., Hassell, 1998; Walter, 2002; Walter & Hassell, 2000; Yap, Douglas, Railsback, Shaughnessy, & Speth, 2000).

While studies suggest that externally developed school reform models or "promising programs" have advantages over locally developed reforms in systemically raising students' academic achievement (Herman et al., 1999; Nunnery, 1998; Stringfield, Millsap, & Herman, 1997), the importance of "co-construction" and ownership of the reform by those principals and teachers engaged in implementing it has also been highlighted (Datnow, Hubbard, & Mehan, 1998, 2002). District central offices will continue to experience a tension when choosing between externally developed reform models and more locally developed initiatives, or they may so adapt externally developed models to the local situation that the reform developers are tempted to disown them (depending on student achievement results).

Supporting Good Instructional Practice

Once decisions have been made about what curriculum and instructional practices to put into place, the issue of "how to get it done" (Corcoran et al., 2001)—supporting good instructional practice and coordinating the curricular decisions—comes to the fore. Again, advocates of school-based management would leave this function to the school leader, who would analyze the professional development needs of the staff and could choose to purchase services from outside vendors as well as from the central office. But this begs the question of how schools acquire leaders who will know how to support good instructional practice and faculties who will implement it. As Spillane and Thompson (1997) pointed out, a primary issue for the school district is one of human capital. How are personnel recruited in the first place? How are principals developed as leaders? And how are teachers helped to deliver excellent instruction?

High-Reliability Recruitment of Principals and Teachers

Numerous studies have addressed the crucial need for district central offices to play a more effective role in recruiting both principals and teachers. As Stringfield (1997) pointed out, school districts need to learn from the best of the organizations that recruit extensively. Research has demonstrated that districts often lose more highly qualified candidates because of "inadequate management systems and cumbersome hiring procedures that discourage good applicants by large numbers of steps in the application process, demeaning treatment, unreturned telephone calls, and lack of timely action" (Darling-Hammond, Berry, Haselkorn, & Fideler, 1999, p. 211; see also Wise, Darling-Hammond, & Berry, 1987; Useem & Farley, 2004). Bureaucratic practices in urban district offices are particularly problematic, creating inefficiencies and delays that cost the district good candidates who take positions elsewhere.

Researchers have noted other central office practices, such as less attention to candidate qualifications (quality of college, college GPA, college major, or credentials) than to other factors (including personal connections), that undermine instructional quality (Browne & Rankin, 1986; Haberman, 1995; Johanson & Gips, 1992; Pflaum & Abrahamson, 1990; Wise et al., 1987). Anderson (1988a) summarized similar problems in districts' recruitment of principals. District practices that assign new teachers to the most challenging classrooms and schools have also undermined their ability to recruit and retain good teachers. Arguing from case study analyses, Snyder (1999) suggested that districts create recruitment systems focused on regional (and even national) colleges, data management systems that make the recruitment process more efficient, and a more welcoming atmosphere that will help to attract high-quality candidates.

Districts also need reliable induction systems for the new faculty and principals they recruit. Darling-Hammond et al. (1999) reported that the traditional "sink-or-swim" situation new teachers found themselves in has improved nationally over the past decade, with more than half of new public school teachers reporting they had experienced some sort of induction program (Darling-Hammond, 1997). But according to research cited by Darling-Hammond, these induction programs tend to offer only the minimum in support to new teachers, and do not distinguish well among the various needs of new teacher graduates, more experienced teachers new to a system, and the various grade levels and subjects of new teachers. The expansion of teacher mentoring programs and professional development schools that participate in the induction process for new teachers is an encouraging sign, but further research is needed about how districts are implementing such programs and what effect they are having on instructional quality and student achievement.

Professional Development for Principals

While effective schools literature established a general consensus about the importance of the principal as instructional leader and linked such instructional leadership to higher student achievement (Teddlie & Reynolds, 2000), it is evident that principals do not become effective instructional leaders automatically (Wimpelberg, 1987). Or as Elmore (2000, p. 2) described it: "Relying on leaders to solve the problem of systemic reform in schools is, to put it bluntly, asking people to do something they don't know how to do and have had no occasion to learn in the course of their careers."

Cuban (1998) pointed out that managerial and political roles have long overshadowed the instructional role of school principals. As Graham (1997) found in a survey of more than 500 principals, the majority of a principal's time is spent in "administrivia." Instructional issues receive only about 5 hours per week, and only a quarter of those surveyed view themselves as instructional leaders. Though some researchers observed that the instructional leader function can be carried out by someone other than the principal (Pajak & Glickman, 1989) or advocated such a position (e.g., Terry, 1996), others have emphasized the need for professional development for principals to help them become more effective in leading instructional improvement and raising student achievement (e.g., Anderson, 1988b). What does the existing literature suggest about the role of the central office in providing such professional development to principals?

Much of the literature linking the central office to principal professional development tends to be advisory, based on authors' long personal experience rather than on systematic research, and often not focused on instructional leadership. These articles touch on issues such as the strengths and weaknesses of principal training programs (Leithwood & Stanley, 1984), principal evaluation and addressing problematic performance (e.g., Bottoni, 1984; Lyman, 1987; Raisch & Rogus, 1995), or training and supporting principals to deal effectively with faculty problems (O'Neil, Riley, & Adamson, 1993; Painter, 2000). Some research studies reported simply on survey data that either directly or indirectly indicates what kind of professional development principals need or want from the central office (e.g., Huinker, Doyle, & Pearson, 1995; Johnson & Snyder, 1990; Poppenhagen, Mingus, & Rogus, 1980); presented a process for central office personnel to determine the professional needs of principals (Geering, 1980; Seagren & Geering, 1980); or effectively evaluate their performance (Duke & Stiggins, 1985; Valentine & Bowman, 1988). Pugh's (1987) case study of a central office initiative to help principals conduct action research found that a district's research and evaluation unit could be useful in facilitating a process of principal reflection that leads to increased levels of instructional leadership and school improvement. Evans and Mohr (1999) also emphasized the importance of the kind of reflective analysis by principals encouraged in action research (including analysis of student work).

We regard the most useful research thus far about the professional development of principals to be found in case studies of districts focused on reform. Fink and Resnick's (1999) case study described the conceptual foundation and process for "developing principals as instructional leaders" undertaken by New York City District #2. Viewing professional development for principals as a "cognitive apprenticeship" aimed at developing nested learning communities of principal, teachers, and students within a school, the District #2 model involves several components:

- monthly day-long conferences for principals on instructional initiatives,
- enrollment in at least one seminar or institute (often provided externally),
- support groups for principals to build leadership skills (principals share problems and get feedback from group),
- principal study groups (focusing on particular instructional practice issues or content areas),
- a "buddy" system to provide peer learning and formalized mentoring for new principals,
- inter-visitation in which principals visit each other's schools, and
- individualized coaching from a central office supervisor involving a supervisory "walkthrough" of the school.

Elmore and Burney (2000) summarized findings from interviews with new principals experiencing the District #2 interventions. Besides the "Aspiring Leaders Program," a fully paid one-year program (combining university coursework with intensive internships with experienced principals) leading to certification for principalship, the new principals experienced a formalized mentoring program during their first year on the job. According to Elmore and Burney (2000), these principals found the support structures much more useful than any formal training in educational administration.

Hightower (2002) and Darling-Hammond et al. (2002) have documented the extension of this model of principal professional development to San Diego. A survey of principals in San Diego found widespread positive reactions to the instructional leadership support structures provided by the district, and considerably more widespread perceptions (compared to a survey of San Francisco Bay Areas principals) that the district was focused on instruction and promoted development for principals and teachers (Darling-Hammond et al., 2002). Though principals suggested ways in which district support could be improved even further, and voiced concern about the higher stakes for principals under this reform effort (15% of principals have been replaced since the reform began), they were still generally supportive of the reforms. While student achievement has risen in District #2 and San Diego, there is no conclusive evidence yet of a causal connection between achievement and efforts to provide professional development for principals.

In comparison, studies of Philadelphia's Children Achieving reform (Christman, 2001; Spiri, 2001) illustrated the need for more focused support structures from the central office to help principals execute their roles as instructional leaders.

The district initiated a support group for 12 principals who were asked to reflect critically on the teaching and learning going on in their schools. These principals voiced a "broad and vague notion of instructional leadership" (Spiri, 2001, p. 16) and had little basis on which to judge their effectiveness. Many viewed the professional development of their staff as the responsibility of the district, possibly because in spite of the school-based management rhetoric associated with the Children Achieving initiative, they still experienced inter- ference and opposition from their district superiors (cluster leaders) when they took any initiative and pursued their own ideas. As Spiri concluded:

> Nowhere in the rhetoric or design of Children Achieving is the essential role of the principal as site-based instructional leader defined or developed. In the absence of clear language about the significance of their role, the principals have been left to make sense of the new structures and instructional imperatives based on their cultural experiences within a District that had func- tioned quite differently than the one conceived in the Children Achieving plan.

Spiri noted that 8 of the 12 principals in the study left the principalship in Philadelphia, and subsequent develop- ments have shown that student achievement levels did not rise enough to forestall the state's decision to turn much of the Philadelphia system over to private groups such as the Edison company (Gewertz, 2002). Similarly, Binkowski,

Corderio, and Iwanicki's (1995) study of two high-performing and two low-performing schools within the same district emphasized the importance of principal leadership in
focusing staff on instructional issues and points to the need
for central office intervention when principals do not exert
this leadership.

Professional Development for Teachers

While virtually no one questions the need to develop human capital among teachers, the issue of the district role
in this process has been subject to much debate. There has
been considerable criticism of the traditional role of the district central office in professional development, especially
when it is bureaucratically organized, generic in approach
and not directly related to the instruction teachers need to
give in the classroom, and treats teachers as passive recipi-
ents of scattershot training rather than active participants
in an ongoing process of training within a community of
learners (Fullan, 1991; Hawley & Valli, 1999). Little (1993)
pointed out that the prevailing training model of professional development for teachers does not fit well with the
contemporary educational reform themes focused on 1)
standards/curriculum/pedagogy, 2) equity, 3) student assessment, 4) social organization of schooling, or 5) professionalization of teaching. Low levels of interaction between
principals and the central office regarding staff development
characterize many schools and districts (Di Natale, 1994).

Some earlier research studies have found that central office supervisors spend more than 40% of their time on activities unrelated to improvement of instruction (Burch & Danley, 1980) or that central office staff are unaware of curriculum and instruction practices at schools in their district (Bogotch & Brooks, 1994; Bogotch, Brooks, MacPhee, & Riedlinger, 1995; Wimpelberg, 1988). Corcoran et al. (2001) found that districts focus on the training process rather than on content in professional development did not appear influenced by research evidence about effective practices. They offered a large variety of training options with no visible focus and did not attempt to evaluate objectively what effect the training had on instructional practice or student achievement. A recent study of a stratified national random sample of 363 districts found a relationship between certain central office management strategies (aligning professional development to standards and assessments, and involving teachers in planning of professional development) and professional development characteristics deemed by recent research studies to be of "higher quality" (e.g., active learning in study groups or networks and collective participation of teachers from same grade/subject area/school). The study did not address the translation of professional development into improved instruction and student achievement (Desimone, Porter, Birmon, Garet, & Yoon, 2002).

> Finding the proper balance for the central office, between being responsive to schools as a "service organization" and playing a more active role of pointing schools in particular staff development directions, has proved particularly important.

Considerably more attention needs to be paid to theories of adult learning and how teachers learn and put into classroom practice what they do learn (Spillane, 2000). As Elmore (1996) has argued, pursuit of large-scale reforms necessitates focused attention on how to motivate teachers to change their practices. Districts need to create the kinds of incentives and support structures that will encourage and enable new teacher learning and changed instructional practice to occur.

The growth of networks linking individual schools sharing common reform designs or funding sources has in some ways sought to replace the district as a source and provider of professional development (Elmore & Burney, 1997). In an era of school-based management, many have observed the need for a transition in the role of the central office from regulator to service provider, particularly in the area of professional development (Asayesh, 1994; Delehant, 1990; Flynn, 1998; Hirsch & Sparks, 1991; Kentta, 1997; Parsley, 1991; Polansky, 1998; Snipes et al., 2002; Wood 1997). A research study of high performing, high poverty schools from various

California districts concluded that the district office support-ed schools in raising student achievement by providing lati-tude and flexibility at the building level and the resources to support needs identified by the school (Rossi, 2000).

It is particularly important to find the proper balance for the central office, between being responsive to schools as a ser-vice organization and playing a more active role of point-ing schools in particular staff development directions. This has been reinforced by research studies that documented unmet professional development and instructional guid-ance needs among both new and more experienced teach-ers and claimed that central office direction would have been useful (Firestone, Rosenblum, & Webb, 1987; Gross-man, Thompson, & Valencia, 2001; Wong, Anagnostopoulos, Routledge, & Edwards, 2001). Organizations such as the National Middle School Association have emphasized the importance of the central office providing "consistent, high-quality professional development for teachers, principals, and parents" (Swaim, 1996, p. 8). But whole-school reform developers have preferred that the district not become too prescriptive in its professional development, allowing flex-ibility for teachers to be trained in the particular curriculum and instructional practices of the model (e.g., Mac Iver & Balfanz, 2000; Slavin & Madden, 1999).

Analysis of a conscious, purposeful central office role in de-veloping human capital among district teachers is probably best illustrated in the case studies of professional development in New York City District #2, which provide a promising framework for the role of the district central office in professional development and evaluating the effectiveness of particular strategies.

Other studies of professional development in District #2 have elaborated some of these principles. Stein, D'Amico, and Israel (1998) found that administrators support literacy instruction by first identifying teachers' instructional needs and providing support. Teachers' needs include more specification about the instructional practice, time for teachers to visit other teachers' classrooms to see practice in action, probing questions of teachers after classroom observation, and help with management issues. They also stressed the need for administrators to help teachers identify unmet student needs and make programmatic adjustments. This model of professional development is focused on classroom practice and individual coaching, and depends on developing common understandings about what good practice is and when children's needs are being met or not. Resnick and Glennan (2001) emphasized that District #2 professional development is linked directly to the instructional program taught by teachers (not generic) and involves on-site coaching and study groups for educators. Several studies of professional development in District #2 have also contributed to our understanding of the importance of content-specific training for teachers and creation of professional communities focused on substantive

Case Study Example:
New York City District #2

Elmore and Burney (1997) summarized the district strategy for professional development as 1) a set of organizing principles about the process of systemic change and the role of professional development in that process, and 2) a set of specific activities, or models of staff development, that focus on systemwide improvement of instruction (p. 6). The organizing principles include a single-minded focus on instruction and recognition that "instructional change is a long, multi-stage process" that needs to take place in a collegial environment in which people work together under a clear set of expectations. In District #2, professional development is not a specialized central office function as it is in many districts, divorced from management and the work setting. Rather, it is "management strategy rather than specialized administrative function. Professional development is what administrative leaders do when they are doing their jobs.... Professional development permeates the work of the organization and the organization of the work" (p. 12). Professional development models used within the district include: 1) the professional development laboratory, 2) instructional consulting services, 3) intervisitation and peer networks, 4) off-site training, and 5) oversight and principal site visits.

knowledge as well as pedagogy (D'Amico et al., 2000; Stein & D'Amico, 1999; Stein et al., 1999). These studies built on other research focused on content-specific issues in professional development (Price, Ball, & Luks, 1995).

This focus on the district-level professional community echoes the work of McLaughlin (1992) and McLaughlin and Talbert (1993) and underscores the social capital component emphasized by Spillane and Thompson (1997). Districts develop social capital by creating a shared culture of instructional improvement, a professional community that extends to relationships with external actors who can increase a shared district knowledge of reform issues and research-backed instructional practices.

Physical Capital/Material Resources

The process of human and social capital development among teachers is closely linked to the physical capital resources available and how districts distribute these among schools. Studies of professional development have emphasized the need for central offices to assure shared planning time for teachers, as well as adequate time for quality professional development (David, 1990; Elmore & Burney, 1999). The District #2 model of professional development requires that principals and lead teachers be freed up from other responsibilities to have the time to spend observing and coaching teachers in their classrooms. Price et al. (1995) have also demonstrated that a district's willingness to "marshal resources for reform" is linked to central office administrators having more than just a surface understanding of the issues in standards-based reform in such subjects as mathematics. In addition, the district office supports (or thwarts) good instructional practice by acquiring and distributing instructional materials and providing budgetary information and flexibility to schools (Cawelti & Protheroe, 2001; Mac Iver & Balfanz, 2000).

Linkages Between Professional Development and Achievement

Since much of the literature on professional development fails to make any linkages to student achievement (Kennedy, 1998), it is not surprising that few studies of the role of the central office in staff development make such a linkage either.[2] One recent study of professional development conducted by central office curriculum specialists among middle grades language arts teachers did include evidence of improved student achievement linked to the efforts of the central office (Confer, 1999). Weathersby and Harkreader (1999) found no direct effect of type of district office leadership on the relationship between staff development and student achievement in their study of low- and high-achieving districts in Georgia. But their findings about the

---

[2] For recent evidence of positive links between professional development and student achievement, see Smith, 2001; Cohen & Hill, 2000; Sherman & Jaeger, 1995; Flecknoe, 2000; Kahle et al., 2000; Langer, 2000.

importance of collaborative planning by teachers and a focus on the classroom and student achievement do suggest issues that need to be emphasized in district office leadership of staff development efforts within schools.

Studies of District #2 have thus far found little direct relationship between the professional development component of the district "model" and student achievement (Harwell et al., 2000; Resnick & Harwell, 2000), though D'Amico et al. (2001) found a moderate relationship between classroom achievement and teachers' perceptions of the quality of professional development in mathematics (the same relationship for reading was not significant). It is possible that more nuanced measurement of the model components and larger, more longitudinal samples will yield more evidence of a relationship in future studies. Fisher (2001) reported evidence of improved student achievement in an inner-city San Diego high school related to the implementation of professional development focused on specific instructional strategies.

Linking Evaluation to District Decision Making

The third component of the central office role—evaluating results and using them to support decision making—often receives the least attention in the literature. This may be attributable to the reality that few districts have research and evaluation offices. Nonetheless, a growing body of research informs our understanding of how districts make use of evaluation in their curricular and instructional decisions. As Corcoran et al. (2001) have emphasized, the need for an evidence-based culture in the district office is essential to measure the effects of reform components on instructional practice and student achievement and ascertaining what changes need to occur to promote increased student achievement. Though the current policy context of increased accountability has forced schools and districts to focus more intently on student achievement data, the CPRE comparative district study has pointed out the need for greater cohesion between evaluation research and central office policy making.

The Center for the Study of Evaluation (CSE) studies of school district research offices, now more than two decades old, laid the foundation for research understanding of the link between district office evaluation efforts and student achievement. The seminal pioneering work of Lyon, Doscher, McGranahan, and Williams (1978, 1979), the "Evaluation and School Districts Project," sought to identify factors that contributed to the research office's participation in instructional change (the intermediary factor influencing student achievement). As Williams and McGranahan (1983) pointed out, however, the CSE studies uncovered "considerable evidence that in many school districts, evaluation units have never played a very significant role in local school district decision making, in spite of their potential to do so" (p. 2). Before increased accountability pressures, even the use of standardized test data by central office administrators was limited (David, 1978; Sproull & Zubrow, 1981a, 1981b), though the institution of mandatory statewide testing and stricter accountability measures resulted in greater central office attention to test results and curriculum definition (Corbett & Wilson, 1987; Corbett & Wilson, 1989). Institutional or organizational impediments to the use of evaluation data to inform school and district policy were found in studies by Daillak (1980), Grusky (1980), O'Reilley (1980), and O'Shea (1980), though creative evaluators could pursue their goals of instructional improvement through informal means and channels.

Kennedy's (1983) study of 16 school districts provides a thorough analysis of the role of evaluators in the central office. School districts' management and decision making practices influenced the role of the evaluator and therefore influence the creation and use of evaluation data. Kennedy found that evaluators' roles were shaped by who they serve and the services they provide. Because decision making can occur in the classroom, in the school, in the central office, by the superintendent, and by the school board, which audience receives the benefits of an evaluator's service will affect their role and services rendered. The most commonly reported responsibilities, and those which consumed most evaluators' time, were administering testing programs and conducting mandated evaluations. Additionally, whether policy makers were concerned with program effectiveness or concerned with the performance of individual teachers and principals shaped the responsibilities and functions of the evaluation staff. For instance, those concerned with program effectiveness were required to produce summative evaluations, while those focusing on staff performance were responsible for providing accountability data. Kennedy's study ultimately illustrated how school districts generate evaluation and other data, as well as how that information is interpreted and used in decision making. However, Kennedy's analysis also exposed some of the challenges inherent in the school districts' evaluation function.

Several studies uncovered differential levels of evaluation use, contributing to a deeper understanding of the issues involved in linking evaluation to school improvement policy making and student achievement. Stecher, Alkin, and Flesher (1981) qualified their conclusion that "school decision makers did not frequently rely upon evaluation when they made decisions" (p. 122) by emphasizing that evaluation data played a more important role in the "problem recognition" stage of the broader decision making process. This study, along with the work of Pechman and King (1986), examined different types and levels of evaluation use among different sets of actors within the school system. Other researchers articulated ways to address particular issues in the evaluation process to promote greater use of evaluation in school decision making, including providing opportunities for greater collaboration between the district research office staff and teachers, and assuring that results are presented in a timely and user-friendly

> Evaluation is an inherently contradictory activity. Evaluators are expected to facilitate change, yet clients resist change. Evaluators are expected to help organizations achieve goals, yet because organizations may consist of parts whose goals are incompatible, helping one group may entail hindering another. Evaluators are expected to produce decision-oriented information, yet clients can rarely identify decision options far enough in advance to make it possible to study them. Evaluators are often expected to observe organizational activities from an objective position, yet their credibility may depend on being perceived as sympathetic friends. Most of these tensions are inherent in the task of evaluation (Kennedy, 1983, p. 519).

manner (Burry & Alkin, 1984; Burry, Alkin, & Ruskus, 1985; Herman, 1985; Lewis, 1985; McDaid & Davis, 1991; Mitroff, 1982; West & Rhoton, 1994).

Researchers identified several factors that inhibited districts from focusing on the link between evaluation and instruction. As these researchers pointed out, school districts were not being pressured in the early 1980s (before the current era of high stakes accountability systems) to consider the link between instruction and student test scores, and both teachers and administrators were inclined to attribute lower scores to student demographics rather than to instructional variables. At the same time, researchers also identified factors shared by districts that were seeking to systematically link evaluation and analysis of student achievement to instructional practice.

Some studies of districts with a focused link between the evaluation office and instructional improvement efforts reported evidence of improvement in student achievement, though it was problematic to infer causality (e.g., Crabbe, Swainston, & Williams, 1983) and the reports were sometimes based on district perceptions that had not been independently confirmed (e.g., Swainston, 1982; Williams & Bank, 1982). Besides the studies cited above, ERIC and related searches uncovered few other citations regarding research or evaluation at the central office level of the school system, much less research studies showing any impact of this on student achievement. Several case studies of research and evaluation offices offered descriptive details of the creation of such offices (Berry, 1985), models of systematic administration of standardized tests (Matter & Ligon, 1983), technical assistance to schools in the process of restructuring or conducting planning for improvement (Borton, 1990; Crawford & Purser, 1988), support for action research (Pugh, 1987), and recommendations (based on surveys of principals and teachers) for how such offices can help support school improvement (Claus & Chen, 1982; Knudson & Wood, 1998). Other studies advocated practices for evaluation offices, such as establishing effective feedback loops

Factors Inhibiting the Link Between Evaluation and Instruction

1) Rapidly Changing Environmental Conditions—changes in student population, staffing, budget levels

2) Permeable Boundaries—pressures from outside interests that took precedence over pursuit of instructional excellence

3) Loose Coupling—weak linkages between individual classrooms and schools and central office decision making structures, resulting in teacher isolation

4) Goal Ambiguity—the district's inability to formulate specific enough goals to be able to link instruction and assessment

5) A "Weak Technical Core"—paucity of research studies linking learning outcomes to instructional methods

(Bank, 1981; Bank & Willams, 1983; Weick, 1976, 1882; Williams & Bank, 1982a, 1982b, 1983).

Factors Supporting the Link Between Evaluation and Instruction

1) Existence of district leaders who believed in making this link, what Williams and Bank (1982a, 1982b) referred to as "idea champions."

2) A stable core group of administrators (staff turnover was detrimental) and people with a comprehensive rather than ad hoc approach to problem analysis.

3) A tolerance for ambiguity and frustration, since linkage arrangements tend not to develop in a linear fashion but require the merging of independent components.

As Williams and Bank (1982b) summarized it, the necessary components for this link to occur were ideas (a shared, coherent philosophy of the necessary linkage between instruction and evaluation of student outcomes through testing), operations (technical capacity in computer operations and professional development provision), and coordinating mechanisms (structures to promote communication among the various district offices and principals and classroom teacher). Bank (1981) further identified important central office management strategies that contributed to linking evaluation and instructional practice:

   1) a personnel-improvement-oriented staff development strategy,

   2) a building-oriented problem solving strategy, and

   3) an instructionally-oriented, objectives-based strategy.

regarding testing data between school sites and the central office (Clarke, 1983) and eliminating bottlenecks that affect the timeliness of evaluation reports and their usefulness to decision makers in the school system (Lewis, 1985).

Recent studies (e.g., Bay Area School Reform Collaborative, 2000; Mac Iver & Balfanz, 2000) have pointed out that school districts are often unable to supply schools' need for data or rich data analysis, often because they lack the skilled human resources to do so. Keeney's (1998) Annenberg Challenge Sites report tended to marginalize the role of the district evaluation office, asserting that "typically, such support has been provided by consultants from universities, state departments of education, or educational support groups" (p. 17). Stringfield (1997) has forcefully demonstrated the need for school districts to become "high reliability organizations" that not only build rich databases but also institute processes for assuring that data are considered by policy makers using formal, logical decision analysis.

Though we have been unable to find research studies of district evaluation offices comparable to the CSE studies of two decades ago, several comparative district studies have identified or investigated the processes central offices use to encourage data-driven decision making (Armstrong & Anthes, 2001; Massell, 2000, 2001; Snipes et al., 2002). Massell (2000, 2001) found considerable variation in how districts are promoting the use of data to improve instruction and student achievement, and suggested that the variation was linked more to administrator beliefs about the usefulness of data-based decision making than to the state policy context (degrees of high stakes accountability). Massell also emphasized the continued need to help school leaders acquire and interpret data that will help them to identify what instructional changes need to occur to improve student achievement, an issue also emphasized by Armstrong and Anthes (2001) and Snipes et al. (2002).

After two decades of national movement towards standards-based reform and greater accountability, the 2001 reauthorization of the Elementary and Secondary Education Act, now famous as the No Child Left Behind (NCLB) Act, will undoubtedly have a significant impact on how district offices collect data and interpret results in their efforts to pursue adequate yearly progress (AYP) and improved student achievement (Linn, Baker, & Betebenner, 2002). NCLB requirements for states to use outcome data in the improvement planning process should encourage more studies of how central offices vary in their effectiveness in helping schools to analyze data and draw conclusions about necessary steps in an improvement process. Unfortunately, the increased requirements for testing and reporting yearly progress for many disaggregated groups may encourage districts to take strategic steps unrelated to instructional improvement (such as shaping the testing pool by retention and special education classification or redefining "schools") simply to meet AYP requirements (Goldhaber, 2002). The critical work of studying how districts help schools link test score results more closely to specific instructional variables that influence student achievement remains unexplored.

Chapter Summary: The Research Findings

• Most schools (especially among those serving low-income populations) cannot improve instruction and achievement without some outside help, whether from the district office or some other external partner (whole-school reform program, university school of education, or other education-focused group). Neither charter schools nor school-based management have proved to be a silver bullet as of yet.

• Despite many examples of ineffective district central offices, this structure is a logical source of capacity building for schools to be able to improve instruction and achievement, and there are case study examples of districts that have achieved some level of success in this area. Important areas for capacity building noted in the literature included:
   • advising on good curriculum and instructional practice;
   • recruiting and equipping principals and teachers;
   • helping school staff to analyze data and decide on needed instructional changes; and
   • providing administrative support so that good instruction can occur.

• Most literature about the central office is either mainly descriptive or prescriptive, based on personal experience of the authors. Many of the available research studies tend to focus narrowly on such issues as time use by central office administrators, surveys of what school-based personnel want from the central office, or central office administrators' perspectives on particular reform initiatives.

• Among the most useful recent research studies, there is a great deal of consensus about the importance of:
   • a district culture emphasizing that achievement is the primary responsibility of every staff member in the district and the central office is a support and service organization for the schools;
   • a primary focus on improving instruction, accompanied by a high level of resources devoted to coherent professional development support linked to research-based practices;
   • focused attention on analysis and alignment of curriculum, instructional practice, and assessment; and
   • professional development for principals and teachers in interpreting data to make good instructional decisions.

• The most useful recent research studies tend to fall into three main categories: district outlier studies, district case studies, and comparative district studies. There are particular methodological problems with drawing conclusions from most of these studies:

- District outlier studies have summarized characteristics of high-performing districts, but generally have not made comparisons with central office activity in lower-performing districts.
- District case studies may have longitudinal data over time, but generally have not included data from comparison districts.
- Comparative district studies have generally not yet examined student achievement outcomes.

Chapter 4:

Practical Implications for School Districts

As we consider the practical implications of the link between district central office roles and gains in student achievement, it is useful to focus specifically on what we know to be the most important direct predictors of student achievement. Next to home and family factors, the "teacher qualifications" variable (expertise, knowledge, skill, education, certification, experience) has been shown to explain the most variation in achievement (Armour-Thomas, Clay, Domanico, Bruno, & Allen, 1989; Ferguson, 1991; Greenwald, Hedges, & Laine, 1996; Sanders & Rivers, 1996). Though Darling-Hammond and Ball (1998) cite this body of research to argue primarily for state level policy reforms in the design of teacher education and certification requirements, their recommendations related to recruitment and training of principals, professional development, reward structures for teachers, and organization of the school day point out numerous important roles for central office administrators (at least until their goal of significantly higher professionalization of the teaching force is achieved and capacity-building from the district may no longer be needed at most schools).

This link between teacher qualifications and student achievement assumes an intermediary variable, "quality of classroom instruction," that is the direct predictor of achievement. This conception of the intermediary variable is a simplification of the model proposed by Stringfield (1994) that builds on the work of Slavin (1987) and posits a four-part "QAIT" (quality, appropriateness, incentive, and time of instruction) with the following components: regular classroom, compensatory education, special programs, and additional input from parents at home. We include "opportunity to learn" measures under this overarching umbrella of "quality of classroom instruction."

A Model of the Central Office Role in Student Achievement

Figure 1 shows a proposed model to guide future research and practice. It expands the school and district components of the Stringfield (1994) model to include several school/classroom-level variables either shown or posited by earlier research to influence the quality of classroom instruction (a variable that is difficult to measure directly on a large scale because of the labor intensity of classroom observation research), together with district-level variables shown by this review to influence the school/classroom variables. School/classroom level predictors of the quality of classroom instruction include: teacher qualifications (degree, certification, years of experience, etc.), quality of professional development experienced by teachers, quality of curricular materials used in the classroom, and instructional leadership from the principal.

The district-level practices that influence each of these variables in the model include those issues highlighted in the review of the literature. Decision making functions consist of the selection and alignment of curriculum and instruction across the district, as well as the possible adoption of externally developed whole-school reform packages. The district role in supporting good instructional practices includes hiring practices for teachers and principals, curriculum and instructional guidance and materials provided to schools and teachers, district support to principals in their instructional leadership role, and the district role in assuring that teachers receive quality professional development tailored to increase the quality of their classroom instruction (see Figure 1). Finally, central offices can evaluate results and use the feedback to evaluate decision making and instructional practice, which supports instruction and achievement through the development and use of results that inform and improve both decision making on curricular and instructional guidance.

Figure 1. Models of Variables Influencing Student Achievement at the Classroom, School, and District Level

DISTRICT LEVEL	SCHOOL/CLASSROOM LEVEL	STUDENT LEVEL

Decision Making on Curriculum and Instruction

- Selection and alignment of curriculum/instructional practices and provisions of curricluar guidance
- Selection of externally developed reform programs

→ Curriculum being used and materials available (opportunity to learn)

Teacher qualifications

Principal qualifications

Supporting Good Instructional Practice

- Hiring Practices
- District Support to Principals
- District Support for Teacher Professional Development

→ Instructional leadership from principal

→ Teachers receive appropriate professional development geared at improving classroom instruction

→ Quality of classroom instruction → Student achievement

Evaluating Results and Feedback Loop

- Structures in place for data collection on implementation (not just achievement) and ensuring usage of findings in feedback loop for decision making

District staff works with teachers and principals to measure:
- Implementation of curriculum and instruction
- Participation in and impact of professional development
- Effectiveness of hiring practices
- Effectiveness of other central office support mechanisms

District efforts in measuring and evaluating practices influence quality of classroom instruction and student achievement indirectly through feedback loops to district decision making and supports for good instructional practice

The model in Figure 1 presents the mechanics of how central office activities can and do shape instruction and student achievement. Although full operationalization of this model is beyond the scope of this review, we suggest various ways of examining district functions in a practical way (see Table 4.1). Like the theoretical model, district functions are categorized into decision making, supports for good instructional practices, and the use of evaluation. In addition, a set of questions pertaining to these functions is provided. These questions can be used to prompt researchers or practitioners to explore more closely their districts' activities in relation to instruction and achievement.

Implications for Practitioners

This model and the corresponding questions in Table 4.1 provide a useful framework for district leaders and other practitioners. District leaders need to consider and evaluate all central office functions and practices in their relationship to support effective instructional practice. This involves creating mechanisms to ensure that district leaders are posing these questions and collecting the necessary information to assure that answers are available and progress over time can be measured. We present a potential feedback loop model for such a process.

Table 4.1. Evaluating District Level Function

District Role	Specific Function	Indicators
Decision making about curriculum/ instruction	Selection and alignment of curriculum and instructional practices	To what extent does the district: • Assure that the curriculum, instruction, and assessment are aligned? • Make decisions about textbook/ curriculum adoptions based on evidence of effectiveness? • Provide assistance to schools in selecting curriculum appropriate for their students and teachers? • Provide materials to schools in a timely fashion? • Provide detailed guides to schools and teachers about how to use the curriculum? • Support principals and teachers on how to meet performance goals and standards using the curriculum?
	Adoption of externally developed reforms	To what extent does the district: • Select reform models based on evidence of effectiveness? • Provide continued support for program implementation? • Provide materials to schools in a timely fashion?
Supporting good instructional practice	Hiring practices	To what extent does the district: • Use sophisticated information technology in personnel systems? • Advertise positions widely (including through the Web site)? • Engage in recruitment efforts at colleges of education? • Set high standards for teacher quality? • Emphasize and execute "welcoming" policies in recruiting new staff? • Make hiring decisions early (in comparison to surrounding districts)? • Maintain a database of qualifications of applicants and new hires? • Analyze the outcomes of hiring practices and make changes to increase the qualifications of teachers hired?

Table 4.1. Evaluating District Level Function *(continued)*

District Role	Specific Function	Indicators
Supporting good instructional practices, continued	Support to principals	To what extent does the district provide: • Mentoring programs for new principals? • Hands-on guidance from the central office supervisor? • Professional development in how to be an instructional leader? • Professional development in how to use data to improve instruction? • Relevant student data in a timely fashion? • Relevant budget information in a timely fashion? • Relief from bureaucratic demands that take time away from instructional leadership?
	Professional development support to teachers	To what extent does the district provide support for: • Mentoring programs for new teachers? • Professional development linked to specific curriculum and textbooks used? • Follow-up, including hands-on guidance from central office staff or highly qualified coaches? • Time for teachers to observe master teachers, talk with colleagues about instructional issues, and reflect on learning to better put it into practice? • Instruction in how to use data from classroom assessments to improve instruction?
Evaluating results and the feedback loop from evaluation to decision making	District measurement of implementation of curriculum and instruction	To what extent does the district: • Evaluate the effectiveness of different curricular/instructional practices in the district? • Have structures/processes in place for the collection of data on implementation (not just assessment of student achievement)? • Have structures or processes for ensuring the use of findings or feedback in their curricular and instructional decisions?
	District measurement of participation in and impact of professional development	

A District Policy Making, Feedback Loop Process

- Create an interdepartmental task force of senior level staff "idea champions" accountable to the CEO who are committed to effecting change to improve central office operations influencing factors associated with student achievement
- Task force identifies key needs for change (e.g., How do HR practices keep districts from increasing the number of highly qualified teachers needed to provide high-quality instruction for improved student achievement?)
- Collect data relevant to issue task force given authority by the CEO over district resources to obtain necessary data (e.g., survey of new teachers and applicants who did not accept positions to determine issues requiring action)
- Analyze data and discuss implications (e.g., high levels of negative feedback regarding loss of transcripts and failure to respond to phone calls indicate need for staff action to reduce these obstacles)
- Create action plan (e.g., plan "service orientation" training for HR staff and production goals for dealing with prospective applicants)
- Prepare for implementation
- Implement the prescription
- Monitor implementation
- Evaluate progress
- Continue improvement process cycle with revised identification of needs for change

(adapted from Blum and Butler, 1987, "Onward to Excellence: 10-Step Process for Cyclical School Improvement", Northwest Regional Educational Laboratory).

Implications for Researchers

The model in Figure 1 suggests a number of empirical analyzes that would expand and deepen our understanding of the impact central offices can have on student achievement. A number of studies have addressed the relationship between district activities and school/classroom factors, such as principal and teacher qualifications, curriculum, and reform packages. However, as noted throughout this review, there are few studies which draw direct relationships from district functions to either the quality of classroom instruction or student achievement. Our model pushes further, seeking to understand this relationship. Table 4.1 offers possible ways to operationalize district functions. In addition, a more complex model would also include factors influencing district practices, such as state or union policies related to hiring practices, financial resources available, quality of central office staff, and the political context (state, local community, school board, etc.) influencing district decisions (e.g., Land, 2002). We leave it to others to begin the process of operationalizing those contextual variables surrounding district practices.

Researchers could then examine one or more linkages in this proposed model. For example, one could collect data about the hiring practices of several districts over time and analyze how variation in hiring practices is related to variation in new teacher qualifications and ultimately student achievement. Ideally, research studies would examine the combination of district level practices, given research that has previously suggested that it is the combination of practices (not any one in isolation) that leads to improved student achievement (Snipes et al., 2002).

Given the significant amount of discussion in current literature about "data-driven instruction," it would also be useful to conduct a comparative study of district office evaluation and research units, building on the prior work at the Center for the Study of Evaluation and the recent work of Armstrong and Anthes (2001), Massell (2001), and Snipes et al. (2002). What kinds of evaluation reports do these offices produce and how are these used at the school level to improve instruction and student achievement? What activities do these units within the central office conduct to build capacity at the school level to collect and interpret data in a way that facilitates instructional improvement and improved student achievement? How are variations in this type of district-level activity related to variation in student achievement and achievement gains across districts?

Methodologically speaking, studies of the impact of central office activities on student achievement need to examine the problems in measurement and devise better measures of the intervention variables as well as additional measures of the achievement outcome variables. It is also essential that these studies become more longitudinal and examine a wider range of grade levels. Inclusion of comparable analyses of data from comparison districts not engaged in the activist central office level reforms is another essential component for further research on central office influences on student achievement.

What We Have Learned

What have we learned from this literature review about the role of the central office in improving instruction and student achievement?

- Those who seek to reduce or eliminate the role of a central office can indeed cite many examples of how individual schools (including charter schools) have improved instruction and student achievement without the direct help of a central office. But many of the external partners who have helped schools achieve these results do point out ways in which central office logistical support is crucial for continued success.

- Despite the much heralded success stories of individual schools, most schools (especially among those serving low-income populations) cannot improve instruction and achievement without some outside help, whether from the central office or some other external partner (whole-school reform program, university school of education, or other education-focused group). Neither charter schools nor SBM have proved to be a silver bullet.

• Most literature about the central office is either mainly descriptive or prescriptive, based on personal experience of the authors.

• Many of the available research studies tend to focus narrowly on such issues as time use by central office administrators, surveys of what school-based personnel want from the central office, or central office administrators' perspectives on particular reform initiatives.

• Among the most useful recent research studies, there appears to be consensus about the importance of:
   1) a district culture emphasizing that achievement is the primary responsibility of every staff member in the district and the central office is a support and service organization for the schools;
   2) a primary focus on improving instruction, accompanied by a high level of resources devoted to coherent professional development linked to research-based practices;
   3) focused attention on analysis and alignment of curriculum, instructional practice and assessment; and
   4) professional development for principals and teachers in interpreting data to make good instructional decisions.

• There are some promising attempts to link individual level student achievement to variations in how classroom teachers and school principals have experienced central office reform activities (professional development strategies, etc.), but more longitudinal research is essential.

As this review has shown, calls for the "demise" of the central office appear largely premature. While there are certainly numerous examples of ineffective central offices, those who advocate doing away with them altogether have yet to propose solutions that will raise achievement in more than a small group of schools in any geographic area (and, in particular, in the many urban areas of the country). This review has highlighted a growing body of research that seeks to identify central office characteristics that distinguish districts effective at raising student achievement from those that are not. While there is considerably more research activity to be conducted before we can draw more than preliminary conclusions, it is time to bring the district back into the mainstream of research on school reform—even if such research cannot be conducted according to the randomized study designs that have become the standard for educational researchers. If a key determinant of student achievement is the quality of instruction received by the student, researchers must continue to investigate how the quality of instruction can be increased in as many classrooms as possible. While a degree of school level autonomy is essential in improving instruction for students, and recentralization is certainly not the answer, the role of the central office in positively influencing those factors that raise the quality of classroom instruction cannot be ignored.

References

Anderson, M. W. (1988a). Hiring capable principals: How school districts recruit, groom, and select the best candidates. *OSSC Bulletin, 31*(9), 40.

Anderson, M. W. (1988b). Inducting principals: How school districts help beginners succeed. *OSSC Bulletin, 32*(2), 63.

Annenberg Institute for School Reform. (2002). *District redesign*. Retrieved on September 17, 2002 from http://www.annenberginstitute.org/issues/district_framework.html

Armour-Thomas, E., Clay, C., Domanico, R., Bruno, K., & Allen, B. (1989). *An outlier study of elementary and middle schools in New York City: Final report*. New York: New York City Board of Education.

Armstrong, J., & Anthes, K. (2001). How data can help. *American School Board Journal, 188* (11), 38-41.

Asayesh, G. (1994). The changing role of central office and its implications for staff development. *Journal of Staff Development, 15*(3), 2-5.

Bank, A. (1981). *School district management strategies to link testing with instructional change* (CSE Rep. No. 168). Los Angeles: University of California, Graduate School of Education and Information Studies, Center for the Study of Evaluation.

Bank, A., & Williams, R. C. (1983). *School district use of testing and evaluation for instructional decision making: A beginning* (CSE Rep. No. 204). Los Angeles: University of California, Graduate School of Education and Information Studies, Center for the Study of Evaluation.

Barth, P. (1994). From crisis to consensus: Setting standards in Chicago. *Perspective, 7*(1), 21.

Bay Area School Reform Collaborative. (2001). *Turning Point: Annual report*. San Francisco: Author.

Berends, M., Kirby, S. N., Naftel, S., & McKelvey, S. (2001). *Implementation and performance in New American Schools three years into scale-up*. Santa Monica, CA: RAND Corporation.

Berg, J., Hall, G., & Difford, G. (1996). Is downsizing the route to rightsizing or capsizing? *The School Administrator, 53*(6), 23-26.

Berkeley, M. (2002). The importance and difficulty of disciplined adherence to the educational reform model. *Journal of Education for Students Placed at Risk, 7*(2), 221-239.

Berne, R., Fine, M., Fruchter, N., Lauber, D., Lewis, H., Palaich, R., et al. (1995). *Reinventing central office: A primer for successful schools*. Chicago: Cross City Campaign for Urban School Reform.

Berry, R. (1985, March). *Decentralization of decision making in Riverside, California: Some of the why and the how from the superintendent's viewpoint*. Paper presented at the annual meeting of the American Educational Research Association, Chicago.

Beyer, F. S., & Houston, R. L. (1988). *Assessment of school needs for low achieving students: Staff survey*. Philadelphia, PA: Research for Better Schools.

Biester, T. W., et al. (1983). *A field test of Achievement Directed Leadership. Documentation Report: Phase II*. Philadelphia: Research for Better Schools.

Biester, T. W., Kruss, J., Meyer, F., & Heller, B. (1984, April). *Effects of administrative leadership on student achievement*. Paper presented at the annual meeting of the American Educational Research Association, New Orleans, LA.

Binkowski, K., Cordeiro, P., & Iwanicki, E. (1995, April). *A qualitative study of higher and lower performing elementary schools.* Paper presented at the annual conference of the American Educational Research Association, San Francisco.

Blum, R. E., & Butler, J. A. (1987, April). *"Onward to excellence": Teaching schools to use effective schooling and implementation research to improve student performance.* Paper presented at the annual meeting of the American Educational Research Association, Washington, DC.

Bodilly, S. J. (1998). *Lessons from New American Schools' scale-up phase: Prospects for bringing designs to multiple schools.* Santa Monica, CA: RAND Corporation.

Bodilly, S. J., & Berends, M. (1999). Necessary district support for comprehensive school reform. In G. Orfield & E. DeBray (Eds.), *Hard work for good schools: Facts not fads in Title I reform* (pp. 111-119). Cambridge, MA: Harvard University Civil Rights Project.

Bogotch, I. E., & Brooks, C. R. (1994). Linking school level innovations with an urban school district's central office. *Journal of School Leadership, 4*(1), 12-27.

Bogotch, I. E., Brooks, C. R., MacPhee, B., & Riedlinger, B. (1995). An urban district's knowledge of and attitudes toward school-based innovation. *Urban Education, 30*(1), 5-26.

Borton, W. M. (1990, November). *Expanding the evaluation department role in a restructuring district: A technical assistance model.* Paper presented at the annual meeting of the California Educational Research Association, Santa Barbara, CA.

Bottoni, W. R. (1984, March). *How to evaluate and improve the principal's performance.* Paper presented at the annual meeting of the National School Boards Association, Houston, TX.

Brookover, W. B., Beady, C., Flood, P., Schweitzer, J., & Wisenbaker, J. (1979). *School social systems and student achievement: Schools can make a difference.* New York: Praeger Publishers.

Brookover, W. B., & Schneider, J. M. (1975). Academic environments and elementary school achievement. *Journal of Research and Development in Education, 9*(1), 82-91.

Browne, B. A., & Rankin, R. J. (1986). Predicting employment in education: The relative efficiency of national teacher examination scores and student teacher ratings. *Educational and Psychological Measurement, 46*(1), 191-197.

Bryk, A. S., Sebring, P. B., Kerbrow, D., Rollow, S., & Easton J. Q. (1998). *Charting Chicago school reform: Democratic localism as a lever for change.* Boulder, CO: Westview Press.

Bullard, P., & Taylor, B. O. (1993). *Making school reform happen.* Needham Heights, MA: Allyn & Bacon.

Burch, B. G., & Danley, W. E. (1980). The instructional leadership role of central office supervisors. *Educational Leadership, 37*(8), 636-37.

Burry, J., & Alkin, M. C. (1984). *The administrator's role in evaluation use* (CSE Rep. No. 225). Los Angeles: University of California, Graduate School of Education and Information Studies, Center for the Study of Evaluation.

Burry, J., Alkin, M. C., & Ruskus, J. (1985). *Organizing evaluations for use as a management tool* (CSE Rep. No. 242). Los Angeles: University of California, Graduate School of Education and Information Studies, Center for the Study of Evaluation.

Buttram, J. L., Corcoran, T. B., & Hansen, B. J. (1989). *Sizing up your school system: The district effectiveness audit.* Philadelphia: Research for Better Schools.

Cawelti, G., & Protheroe, N. (2001) *High student achievement: How six school districts changed into high-performance systems.* Arlington, VA: Educational Research Service.

Christman, J. B. (2001). *Powerful ideas, modest gains: Five years of systemic reform in Philadelphia middle schools.* Philadelphia: Consortium for Policy Research in Education.

Chubb, J. E., & Moe, T. M. (1990). *Politics, markets, and America's schools.* Washington, DC: Brookings.

Clarke, M. (1983, November). *Functional level testing decision points and suggestions to innovators.* Paper presented at the meeting of the California Educational Research Association, Los Angeles.

Claus, R. N., & Chen, H. (1982). *District-wide evaluation needs assessment study, 1981-82 [and] appendix supplement.* Saginaw, MI: Saginaw Public Schools, Department of Evaluation Services.

Cohen, D., & Hill, H. (2000). Instructional policy and classroom performance: The mathematics reform in California. *Teachers College Record, 102,* 294-343.

Confer, C. (1999). *Interactions between central office language arts administrators and exemplary English teachers, and the impact on student performance.* (CELA research report case study No. 12003). Albany, NY: National Research Center on English Learning and Achievement.

Corbett, H. D., & Wilson, B. L. (1987). *Study of statewide mandatory minimum competency tests.* Philadelphia: Research for Better Schools.

Corbett, H. D., & Wilson, B. L. (1989). *Statewide testing and local improvement: An oxymoron?* Philadelphia: Research for Better Schools.

Corbett, H. D., & Wilson, B. L. (1992). The central office role in instructional improvement. *School Effectiveness and School Improvement, 3*(1), 45-68.

Corcoran, T., & Christman, J. B. (2002). *The limits and contradictions of systemic reform: The Philadelphia story.* Philadelphia: Consortium for Policy Research in Education.

Corcoran, T., Fuhrman, S. H., & Belcher, C. L. (2001). The district role in instructional improvement. *Phi Delta Kappan, 83*(1), 78-84.

Corcoran, T., & Wilson, B. L. (1986). *The search for successful secondary schools: The first three years of the Secondary School Recognition Program.* Philadelphia: Research for Better Schools.

Crabbe, L., Swainston, T., & Williams, R. C. (1983). *How two evaluation offices help improve school performance* (CSE Rep. No. 203). Los Angeles: University of California, Graduate School of Education and Information Studies, Center for the Study of Evaluation.

Crandall, D. P. (1984). School improvement: What the research says. In B.D. Sattes, (Ed.), *Promoting school excellence through the application of effective schools research: Summary and proceedings of a 1984 regional exchange workshop.* Charleston, WV: Appalachia Educational Laboratory.

Crandall, D. P., & Eiseman, J. W. (1983). *Coordinating assistance in school improvement efforts: Issues to consider.* Paper presented at the annual meeting of the American Educational Research Association, Montreal, Quebec, Canada.

Crawford, J., & Purser, S. (1988). Perspectives on school-based planning. *Educational Planning, 7*(2), 18-32.

Cross City Campaign for Urban School Reform. (2002). *About us.* Retrieved on December 16, 2002 from http://www.crosscity.org/about/index.htm

Crowson, R. L., & Boyd, W. L. (1992). Urban schools as organizations: Political perspectives. In J. Cibulka, R. Reed, & K. Wong (Eds.), *Politics of Education Association Yearbook 1991. The politics of urban education in the United States* (pp. 87-104). Washington DC: The Falmer Press.

Crowson, R. L., & Morris, V. C. (1985). Administrative control in large-city school systems: An investigation of Chicago. *Educational Administration Quarterly, 21,* 51-70.

Cuban, L. (1984). Transforming the frog into the prince: Effective schools research, policy, and practice at the district level. *Harvard Educational Review, 54*(2), 129-50.

Cuban, L. (1998). How schools change reforms: Redefining reform success and failure. *Teachers College Record, 99,* 453-477.

Cushman, K. (1991). Creating a climate for change: Essential schools in Louisville. *Horace 7*(5). Retrieved on November, 25, 2002 from http://www.essentialschools.org/cs/resources/view/ces_res/100

D'Amico, L., Harwell, M., Stein, M. K., & van den Heuvel, J. (2001). *Examining the implementation and effectiveness of a district-wide instructional improvement effort.* Paper presented at the annual meeting of the American Educational Research Association, Seattle, WA.

D'Amico, L., & Stein, M. K. (1999). *The role of performance standards in the enactment of literacy instruction.* Paper presented at the annual meeting of the American Educational Research Association, Montreal, Canada.

D'Amico, L., van den Heuvel, J., & Harwell, M. (2000). *Perspectives on instructional improvement in literacy and mathematics.* Pittsburgh, PA: University of Pittsburgh, HPLC Project, Learning Research and Development Center.

Daillak, R. H. (1980). *A field study of evaluators at work* (CSE Rep. No. 154). Los Angeles: University of California, Graduate School of Education and Information Studies, Center for the Study of Evaluation.

Darling-Hammond, L. (1997). *Doing what matters most: Investing in quality teaching.* New York: National Commission on Teaching and America's Future.

Darling-Hammond, L. (1999). *Teacher quality and student achievement: A review of state policy evidence.* (Document R-99-1). Seattle, WA: University of Washington, Center for the Study of Teaching and Policy.

Darling-Hammond, L., & Ball, D. L. (1998). *Teaching for high standards: What policymakers need to know and be able to do* (CPRE joint report series). Philadelphia: Consortium for Policy Research in Education.

Darling-Hammond, L., Berry, B. T., Haselkorn, D., & Fideler, E. (1999). Teacher recruitment, selection, and induction: Policy influences on the supply and quality of the teachers. In L. Darling-Hammond & G. Sykes (Eds.), *Teaching as the learning profession: Handbook of policy and practice* (pp. 183-232). San Francisco: Jossey-Bass Publishers.

Darling-Hammond, L., Hightower, A. M., Husbands, J. L., LaFors, J. R., & Young, V. M. (2002, April). *Building instructional quality: Inside-out, bottom-up, and top-down perspectives on San Diego's school reform.* Paper presented at the annual meeting of the American Educational Research Association, New Orleans, LA.

Datnow, A., Borman, G., & Stringfield, S. (2000). School reform through a highly specified curriculum: Implementation and effects of the Core Knowledge Sequence. *Elementary School Journal, 101*(2), 167-191.

Datnow, A., & Castellano, M. (2003). District and school leadership in Success for All schools. In J. Murphy & A. Datnow (Eds.), *Leadership for school reform: Lessons from comprehensive school reform designs,* (pp. 127-162). Thousand Oaks, CA: Corwin Press.

Datnow, A., Hubbard, L., & Mehan, H. (1998). *Educational reform implementation: A co-constructed process* (Research Rep. No. 5). Santa Cruz, CA: Center for Research on Education, Diversity, and Excellence.

Datnow, A., Hubbard, L., & Mehan, H. (2002). *Extending educational reform: From one school to many.* New York: Routledge Falmer.

Datnow, A., & Stringfield, S. (2000). Working together for reliable school reform. *Journal of Education for Students Placed At Risk, 5*(1-2) 183-204.

David, J. L. (1978). Local uses of Title I evaluations. *Education Evaluation and Policy Analysis, 3*(1), 27-39.

David, J. L. (1990). Restructuring in progress: Lessons from pioneering districts. In R. Elmore, et al. (Eds.), *Restructuring schools: The next generation of educational reform,* (pp. 209-250). San Francisco: Jossey-Bass Publishers.

Davidson, B. M. (1993, January). *The influence of the central office on school restructuring: A study of selected accelerated schools.* Paper presented at the annual meeting of the Southwest Educational Research Association, Austin, TX.

Delehant, A. M. (1990). A central office view: Charting a course when pulled in all directions. Personal reflections of shared decision-making. *The School Administrator, 47*(8), 14, 17-19.

Desimone, L., Porter, A. C., Birmon, B. F., Garet, M. S., & Yoon, K. S. (2002). How do school districts affect the quality of professional development provided to teachers? Results from a national sample of districts. *Teachers College Record, 104*(7), 1265-1312.

DiNatale, J. J. (1994). School improvement and restructuring: A three-fold approach. *NASSP Bulletin, 78*(564), 79-83.

Doyle, D. P., & Pimental, S. (1993). A study in change: Transforming the Charlotte-Mecklenburg schools. *Phi Delta Kappan, 74,* 534-539.

Duke, D. L., & Stiggins, R. J. (1985). Evaluating the performance of principals: A descriptive study. *Educational Administration Quarterly, 21*(4), 71-98.

Dusewicz, R. A. & Beyer, F. S. (1991). *Dimensions of excellence scales: Survey instruments for school improvement.* Philadelphia: Research for Better Schools.

Edmonds, R. (1979). Effective schools for the urban poor. *Educational Leadership, 37*(1), 15-24.

Effron, R. C., & Concannon, J. P. (1995). Rightsizing the right way. *The School Administrator, 52*(3), 40-41, 43, 45, 47.

Elmore, R. F. (1993). The role of local school districts in instructional improvement. In S. Fuhrman (Ed.), *Designing coherent education policy: Improving the system* (pp. 96-124). San Francisco: Jossey-Bass Publishers.

Elmore, R. F. (1996). Getting to scale with successful educational practices. In S. Fuhrman & J. O'Day (Eds.), *Rewards and reform: Creating educational incentives that work* (pp. 294-329). San Francisco: Jossey-Bass Publishers.

Elmore, R. F. (2000). *Building a new structure for school leadership.* Washington, DC: Albert Shanker Institute.

Elmore, R. F., & Burney, D. (1997). *School variation and systemic instructional improvement in Community School District #2, New York City.* Pittsburgh, PA: University of Pittsburgh, HPLC Project, Learning Research and Development Center.

Elmore, R. F., & Burney, D. (1998). *Continuous improvement in Community School District #2, New York City.* Pittsburgh, PA: University of Pittsburgh, HPLC Project, Learning Research and Development Center.

Elmore, R. F., & Burney, D. (1999). Investing in teacher learning. In L. Darling-Hammond and G. Sykes (Eds.), *Teaching as the learning profession,* (pp. 263-291). San Francisco: Jossey-Bass Publishers.

Elmore, R. F., & Burney, D. (2000). *Leadership and learning: Principal recruitment, induction, and instructional leadership in Community School District #2, New York City.* Pittsburgh, PA: University of Pittsburgh, HPLC Project, Learning Research and Development Center.

Eubanks, E. E., & Levine, D. U. (1983). A first look at effective schools projects in New York City and Milwaukee. *Phi Delta Kappan, 64*(10), 697-702.

Evans, P. M., & Mohr, N. (1999). Professional development for principals: Seven core beliefs. *Phi Delta Kappan, 80*(7), 530-32.

Fairman, J. C., & Firestone, W. A. (2001). The district role in state assessment policy: An exploratory study. In S. Fuhrman (Ed.), *From the capitol to the classroom: Standards-based reform in the states. One hundredth yearbook of the National Society for the Study of Education Part II* (pp. 124-147). Chicago: The University of Chicago Press.

Ferguson, R. (1991). Paying for public education: New evidence on how and why money matters. *Harvard Journal of Legislation, 28,* 465-498.

Fink, E., & Resnick, L. B. (1999). *Developing principals as instructional leaders.* Pittsburgh, PA: University of Pittsburgh, HPLC Project, Learning Research and Development Center.

Finn, C. (1991). *We must take charge: Our schools and our future.* New York: Free Press.

Finnan, C., & Meza, J. (2003). Can a leader change the culture and embed reform? The Accelerated Schools Project in Memphis. In J. Murphy & A. Datnow (Eds.), *Leadership for school reform: Lessons from comprehensive school reform designs,* (pp. 279-314). Thousand Oaks, CA: Corwin Press.

Firestone, W. A., Rosenblum, S., & Webb, A. (1987). *Building commitment among students and teachers: An exploratory study of ten urban high schools.* Philadelphia: Research for Better Schools.

Fisher, D. (2001). Trust the process: Increasing student achievement via professional development and process accountability. *NASSP Bulletin, 85*(629), 67-71.

Fitzgerald, J. H. (1993). Management practices: A profile of district-level supervisory activity in one school district. *Journal of Curriculum and Supervision, 8*(2), 128-39.

Flecknoe, M. (2000). Can continuing professional development for teachers be shown to raise pupils' achievement? *Journal of Inservice Education, 26,* 437-57.

Floden, R., et al. (1984). *Elementary school principals' role in district and school curriculum change.* Paper presented at the annual meeting of the American Educational Research Association, New Orleans, LA.

Floden, R., Porter, A. C., Alford, L. M., Freeman, D. T., Irwin, S., Schmidt, W. H., et al. (1988). Instructional leadership at the district level: A closer look at autonomy and control. *Educational Administration Quarterly, 24,* 96-124.

Flynn, P. (1998). Ready, set, decide! *The School Administrator, 55*(3), 14-16.

Foley, E. (2001, August). *Contradictions and control in systemic reform: The ascendancy of the central office in Philadelphia Schools.* Philadelphia: University of Pennsylvania, Consortium for Policy Research in Education, Graduate School of Education.

French, V. W. (1984, April). *Using research to facilitate implementation: The role of the external linker.* Paper presented at the annual meeting of the American Educational Research Association, New Orleans, LA.

Fullan, M. (1985). Change processes and strategies at the local level. *The Elementary School Journal, 85*(3), 391-421.

Fullan, M. (1991). *The new meaning of educational change.* New York: Teachers College Press.

Geering, A. D. (1980). *A prescriptive model for determining professional development needs of principals.* (ERIC Document Reproduction Service No. ED199929).

Genck, F. H. (1983). *Improving school performance: How new school management techniques can raise learning, confidence, and morale.* New York: Praeger Publishers.

Gewertz, C. (2002). Philadelphia lines up outside groups to run schools. *Education Week, 21*(43), 1, 18, 19.

Goertz, M. E. (2001). Standards-based accountability: Horse trade or horse whip? In S. Fuhrman (Ed.), *From the capitol to the classroom: Standards-based reform in the states. One hundredth yearbook of the National Society for the Study of Education Part II* (pp. 39-59). Chicago: The University of Chicago Press.

Goldhaber, D. (2002). What might go wrong with the accountability measures of the No Child Left Behind Act? *In No Child Left Behind: What will it take?* Paper prepared for a conference sponsored by the Thomas B. Fordham Foundation.

Graeber, A. O., et al. (1984). *Capacity building for a school improvement program, Achievement Directed Leadership.* Philadelphia: Research for Better Schools.

Graham, M. W. (1997, March). *School principals: Their roles and preparation.* Paper presented at the National Conference on Creating the Quality School, Oklahoma City, OK.

Greenwald, R., Hedges, L. V., & Laine, R. D. (1996). The effect of school resources on student achievement. *Review of Educational Research, 66*(3), 361-396.

Grossman, P., Thompson, C., Valencia, S. (2001). *District policy and beginning teachers: Where the twain shall meet.* Seattle, WA: University of Washington Center for the Study of Teaching and Policy.

Grusky, O. (1980). *Role conflict and ambiguity among school district evaluation unit heads* (CSE Rep. No. 140). Los Angeles: University of California, Graduate School of Education and Information Studies, Center for the Study of Evaluation.

Haberman, M. (1995). Selecting 'star' teachers for children and youth in urban poverty. *Phi Delta Kappan, 76*(10), 778-781.

Hall, G. E., Putnam, S., & Hord, S. M. (1985, March). *District office personnel. Their roles and influence on school and classroom change: What we don't know.* Paper presented at the Annual Meeting of the American Educational Research Association, Chicago.

Hall, P. M., & Placier, P. L. (2003). Putting the common principles into practice: Leadership in CES schools, Re: Learning, and the transformation of intentions. In J. Murphy & A. Datnow (Eds.), *Leadership for school reform: Lessons from comprehensive school reform designs* (pp. 315-356). Thousand Oaks, CA: Corwin Press.

Hannaway, J., & Sproull, L. S. (1978-79). Who's running the show? Coordination and control in educational organizations. *Administrator's Notebook, 27*(9), 1-4.

Harwell, M. R., D'Amico, L., Stein, M. K., & Gatti, G. (2000). *Professional development and the achievement gap in Community School District #2.* Pittsburgh, PA: University of Pittsburgh, HPLC Project, Learning Research and Development Center.

Harwell, M. R., & Gatti, G. G. (1999). *The predictors of student achievement in Community School District #2.* Paper presented at the annual meeting of the American Educational Research Association, Montreal, Canada.

Hassell, B. C. (1998). *Comprehensive school reform. Making good choices: A guide for schools and districts.* Oak Brook, IL: North Central Regional Educational Laboratory.

Hawley, W. D., & Valli, L. (1999). The essentials of effective professional development: A new consensus. In L. Darling-Hammond & G. Sykes (Eds.), *Teaching as a Learning Profession: Handbook of Teaching and Policy* (pp. 127-150). San Francisco: Jossey-Bass Publishers.

Helms, D. C., et al. (1985). *Achievement directed leadership: Final report of the basic skills component.* Philadelphia: Research for Better Schools.

Helms, D. C. & Heller, B. (1985). *Using research to improve instructional effectiveness, evolution of Achievement Directed Leadership (ADL).* Paper presented at the annual meeting of the American Educational Research Association, Chicago, IL.

Herman, J. J. (1985). *Local evaluation and school improvement: Current status and future possibilities* (CSE Rep. No. 246). Los Angeles: University of California, Graduate School of Education and Information Studies, Center for the Study of Evaluation.

Herman, R., Aladjem, D., McMahon, P., Massem, E., Mulligan, I., O'Malley, A., et al. (1999). *An educator's guide to schoolwide reform.* Arlington, VA: Educational Research Service.

High Performance Learning Communities Project. (2000). *Annual Report Year 3.* Pittsburgh, PA: University of Pittsburgh, HPLC Project, Learning Research and Development Center.

Hightower, A. (2002). *San Diego's big boom: District bureaucracy supports culture of learning.* Seattle, WA: Center for the Study of Teaching and Policy, University of Washington.

Hill, P. T. (1997). A public education system for the new metropolis. *Education and Urban Society, 29*(4), 490-508.

Hirsh, S., & Sparks, D. (1991). A look at the new central-office administrators. *The School Administrator, 48*(7), 16-17, 19.

Hubbard, L., & Mehan, H. (1999). Educational "niche picking" in a hostile environment. *Journal of Negro Education, 68*(2), 213-226.

Huberman, M. (1981). *ECRI, Masepa, North Plains: Case study.* Andover, MA: The Network.

Huberman, M., & Crandall, D. (1983). *People, policies, and practices: Examining the chain of school improvement: Vol. 9. Implications for action, a study of dissemination efforts supporting school improvement.* Andover, MA: The Network.

Huinker, D., Doyle, L. H., & Pearson, G. E. (1995). *Landscape of mathematics and science education in Milwaukee: A study of the Milwaukee public schools.* Milwaukee, WI: University of Wisconsin Center for Math and Science Education Research.

Johanson, G. A., & Gips, C. J. (1992). The hiring preferences of secondary school principals. *High School Journal, 16,* 1-16.

Johnson, W. L., & Snyder, K. J. (1990, January). *Managing productive schools.* Paper presented at the annual meeting of the Southwest Educational Research Association, Austin, TX.

Johnston, R. C. (2001). Central office is critical bridge to help schools. *Education Week, 20*(25), 1, 18-20.

Jones, C. L., & Hill, C. (1998). Strategy and tactics in subsystem protection: The politics of education reform in Montgomery County, Maryland. In C. N. Stone (Ed.), *Changing urban education* (pp. 139-160). Lawrence, KS: University Press of Kansas.

Kahle, J., Meece, J., & Scantlebury, K. (2000). Urban African-American middle school science students: Does standards-based teaching make a difference? *Journal of Research in Science Teaching, 37,* 1019-41.

Keedy, J. L. (1994). The twin engines of school reform for the 1990s: The school site and national coalitions. *The Journal of School Leadership, 4*(1), 94-111.

Keeney, L. (1998). *Using data for school improvement: Report on the second Practitioners' Conference for Annenberg Challenge Sites.* Providence, RI: Annenberg Institute for School Reform at Brown University.

Kennedy, M. (1998). *The relevance of content in in-service teacher education.* Paper presented at the annual meeting of the American Educational Research Association, San Diego, CA.

Kennedy, M. M. (1983). The role of in-house evaluator. *Evaluation Review, 7*(4), 519-541.

Kentta, B. (1997). The central role in shared decision making. *The School Administrator, 54*(3), 24-26, 28.

Kilgore, S. B., & Jones, J. D. (2003). Leadership in comprehensive school reform initiatives: The case of the Modern Red School House. In J. Murphy & A. Datnow (Eds.), *Leadership for school reform: Lessons from comprehensive school reform designs,* (pp. 52-84). Thousand Oaks, CA: Corwin Press.

Kirby, P. C., & Meza, J. (1995, April). *Coaching versus direct service models for university training to Accelerated Schools.* Paper presented at the annual meeting of the American Educational Research Association, San Francisco.

Klausmeier, H. J. (1985). *A process guide for school improvement* (Program Rep. No. 85-3). Lanham, MD: University Press of America.

Knudson, D. P., & Wood, F. H. (1998). Support from above. *Journal of Staff Development, 19*(3), 27-32.

Kuo, V. (1998). *District office support of school restructuring: Case study results and theoretical implications.* Paper presented at the annual meeting of the American Educational Research Association, San Diego, CA.

Land, D. (2002). Local school boards under review: Their role and effectiveness in relation to students' academic achievement. *Review of Educational Research, 72,* 229-278.

Langer, J. (2000). Excellence in English in middle and high school: How teachers' professional lives support student achievement. *American Educational Research Journal, 37,* 397-439.

Larkin, R. F. (1984, April). *Achievement directed leadership: A superintendent's perspective.* Paper presented at the annual meeting of the American Educational Research Association, New Orleans, LA.

Lasky, S. (2002). The district as lens. In A. Datnow & S. Stringfield (Eds.), *CREDE synthesis project on systemic integration for effective reform.* Unpublished manuscript.

Leithwood, K., Aitken, R., & Jantzi, D. (2001). *Making schools smarter: A system for monitoring school and district progress* (2nd ed.). Thousand Oaks, CA: Corwin Press.

Leithwood, K., & Menzies, T. (1998). A review of research concerning the implementation of site-based management. *School Effectiveness and School Improvement, 9*(3), 233-285.

Leithwood, K., & Stanley, K. (1984). Training principals for school improvement. *Education and Urban Society, 17*(1), 49-71.

Lewis, M. E. (1985, March). *Investigation into the use of time in program evaluation at a school district's department of research and evaluation.* Paper presented at the annual meeting of the American Educational Research Association, Chicago.

Lezotte, L. W., Edmonds, R., & Ratner, G. (1974). *Remedy for school failure to equitably deliver basic school skills: A preliminary research proposal.* Cambridge, MA: Center for Urban Studies, Harvard University.

Lezotte, L. W., Hathaway, D., Miller, S., Passalacqua, J., & Brookover, W. (1980). *School learning climate and academic achievement.* Tallahassee, FL: Florida State University Teacher Education Projects.

Linn, R. L., Baker, E. L., & Betebenner, D. W. (2002). Accountability systems: Implications of requirements of the No Child Left Behind Act of 2001. *Educational Researcher, 31*(6), 3-16.

Little, J. W. (1993). Teachers' professional development in a climate of educational reform. *Educational Evaluation and Policy Analysis, 15*(2), 129-151.

Loucks, S. F., & Cox, P. L. (1982). *School district personnel: A crucial role in school improvement efforts. A study of dissemination efforts supporting school improvement.* Paper presented at the annual meeting of the American Educational Research Association, New York.

Lyman, L. (1987). Hey, central office: Here's how to help principals. *Executive Educator, 9*(3), 27-28.

Lyon, C. D., Doscher, L., McGranahan, P., & Williams, P. (1978). *Evaluation and school districts.* Los Angeles: University of California, Center for the Study of Evaluation.

Lyon, C. D., et al. (1979). *Evaluation offices and instructional renewal. Studies in evaluation and decision making, work unit 1: Evaluation and decision making in school districts.* Los Angeles: University of California, Center for the Study of Evaluation.

Mac Iver, D. J., & Balfanz, R. (2000). The school district's role in helping high-poverty schools become high performing. In B. Gaddy (Ed.), *Including at-risk students in standards-based reform* (pp. 35-69). Aurora, CO: Mid-continent Research for Education and Learning (McREL).

Mac Iver, M. (2003). *Systemic supports for comprehensive school reform: The "institutionalization" of direct instruction in the Baltimore City Public School System.* Paper presented at the annual meeting of the American Educational Research Association, Chicago.

Mac Iver, M., McHugh, B. & Stringfield, S. (2000). *Implementation and effects of the Maryland Core Knowledge Project: Final (fifth year) evaluation report* (Rep. No. 50). Baltimore, MD and Washington, DC: Center for Research on the Education of Students Placed at Risk.

Marsh, J. (2000). *Connecting districts to the policy dialogue: A review of literature on the relationship of districts with states, schools, and communities.* Seattle, WA: University of Washington, Center for the Study of Teaching and Policy.

Massel, D. (2000). *The district role in building capacity: Four strategies.* (CPRE Policy Briefs). Philadelphia: Consortium for Policy Research in Education.

Massel, D. (2001). The theory and practice of using data to build capacity: State and local strategies and their effects. In S. Fuhrman (Ed.), *From the capitol to the classroom: Standards-based reform in the states. One hundredth yearbook of the National Society for the Study of Education Part II* (pp. 148-169). Chicago: The University of Chicago Press.

Matter, M. K., & Ligon, G. (1983, April). *Achievement test preparation: A year-long goal, not a last minute thought.* Paper presented at the annual meeting of the American Educational Research Association, Montreal, Canada.

Mauriel, J. J. (1989). *Strategic leadership for schools: Creating and sustaining productive change.* San Francisco: Jossey-Bass Publishers.

McDaid, J. L., & Davis, D. G. (1991, April). *Program evaluation, curriculum, and testing services implement diverse forms of assessment in the San Diego city schools: A proposed collaboration model.* Paper presented at the annual meeting of the American Educational Research Association, Chicago.

McGrail, J., Wilson, B. L., Buttram, J. L., & Rossman, G. B. (1991). *Looking at schools: Instruments and processes for school analysis.* Philadelphia: Research for Better Schools.

McLaughlin, M. W. (1992). How district communities do and do not foster teacher pride. *Educational Leadership, 50*(1), 33-35.

McLaughlin, M. W., & Talbert, J. E. (1993). *Contexts that matter for teaching and learning: Strategic opportunities for meeting the nation's education goals.* Stanford, CA: Center for Research on the Context of Secondary School Teaching, Stanford University.

Meyer, J., & Rowan, B. (Eds.), (1992). *The structure of educational organizations, organizational environments: Ritual and rationality.* Newbury Park, CA: Sage.

Meyers, H. W., & Sudlow, R. (1992, April). *More effective schools/teaching product: Stalking the fifth claim?* Paper presented at the annual meeting of the American Educational Research Association, San Francisco.

Middleton, J. A., Smith, A. M., & Williams, D. (1994). From directing to supporting school initiatives: One district's efforts. *Journal of Staff Development, 15*(3), 6-9.

Miller, R., Smey-Richman, B., & Woods-Houston, M. (1987). *Secondary schools and the central office: Partners for improvement.* Riverside, CA: University of California.

Mitroff, D. (1982). *Assessing the effects of district testing and evaluation efforts.* (CSE Rep. No. 186). Los Angeles: University of California, Graduate School of Education and Information Studies, Center for the Study of Evaluation.

Mohrman, S. A., Wohlstetter, P. (Eds.), (1994). *School-based management: Organizing for high performance.* San Francisco: Jossey-Bass Publishers.

Murphy, J. (1994). The changing role of the superintendency in restructuring districts in Kentucky. *School Effectiveness and School Improvement, 5*(4), 349-75.

Murphy, J., & Beck, L. (1995). *School-based management as school reform: Taking stock.* Thousand Oaks, CA: Corwin Press.

Murphy, J. & Datnow, A. (2003). Leadership lessons from comprehensive school reform designs. In J. Murphy & A. Datnow (Eds.), *Leadership for school reform: Lessons from comprehensive school reform designs.* Thousand Oaks, CA: Corwin Press.

Murphy, J., & Hallinger, P. (1988). Characteristics of instructionally effective school districts. *Journal of Education Research, 81*(3), 175-181.

Murphy, J., & Shiffman, C. D. (2002). *Understanding and assessing the charter school movement.* New York: Teachers College Press.

Murphy, J. A. (1994). Raising standards in Charlotte-Mecklenburg schools. In C. E Finn & H. J. Walberg (Eds.), *Radical education reforms. The series on contemporary educational issues.* Berkeley, CA: McCutchan Publishing Corporation.

Murphy, J. A. (1995). After forty years: The other half of the puzzle. *Teacher's College Record, 96,* 743-750.

National Commission on Teaching and America's Future. (2002). *District policy inventory.* Retrieved January 9, 2003 from www.nctaf.org/resourcedistrict/policy_inventory1.htm

Nunnery, J. A. (1998). Reform ideology and the locus of development problem in educational restructuring: Enduring lessons from studies of educational innovation. *Education and Urban Society, 30*(3), 277-295.

O'Neil, I. R., & Adamson, D. R. (1993). When teachers falter. *Executive Educator, 15*(1), 25-27.

O'Reilly, C. (1980). *Evaluation information and decision making in organizations: Some constraints on the utilization of evaluation research.* (CSE Rep. No. 142). Los Angeles: University of California, Graduate School of Education and Information Studies, Center for the Study of Evaluation.

Ornstein, A. C. (1989). Administrator/student ratios in large school districts. *Phi Delta Kappan, 70*(10), 806-06.

O'Shea, D. W. (1980). *School district evaluation efforts: Contradictions and implications* (CSE Rep. No. 141). Los Angeles: University of California, Graduate School of Education and Information Studies, Center for the Study of Evaluation.

Painter, S. R. (2000). Easing dismissals and non-renewals. *The School Administrator, 57*(9), 40-43.

Pajak, E. F., & Glickman, C. D. (1989). Dimensions of school district improvement. *Educational Leadership, 46*(8), 61-64.

Parsley, J. F. (1991). Reshaping student learning. *The School Administrator, 48*(7), 9, 11, 13-14.

Pechman, E. M., & King, J. A. (1986, April). *Analyzing the school evaluation use process to make evaluation worth the effort.* Paper presented at the annual meeting of the American Educational Research Association, San Francisco, CA.

Peterson, S. A. (1999). School district central office power and student performance. *School Psychology International, 20*(4), 376-387.

Pflaum, S. W. & Abrahamson, T. (1990). Teacher assignment, hiring, and preparation. *Urban Review, 22*(1), 17-31.

Polansky, H. B. (1998). Equity and SBM: It can be done. *School Business Affairs, 64*(4), 36-37.

Poppenhagen, B., Mingus, J., & Rogus, J. (1980). Comparative perceptions of elementary, junior high, and senior high school principals on selected work related variables. *Journal of Educational Administration, 18*(1), 69-87.

Price, J. N., Ball, D. L., & Luks, S. (1995). *Marshaling resources for reform: District administrators and the case of mathematics.* East Lansing, MI: National Center for Research on Teacher Learning.

Public Schools of North Carolina. (2000). *Improving student performance: The role of district-level staff.* Evaluation brief prepared for the State Board of Education. Raleigh, NC: Evaluation Section, Division of Accountability Services, Public Schools of North Carolina.

Pugh, W. C. (1987, April). *Reflection-in-action as a principal's learning and decision making tool.* Paper presented at the annual meeting of the American Educational Research Association, Washington, DC.

Purkey, S. C., & Smith, M. S. (1983). Effective schools: A review. *Elementary School Journal, 83,* 427-452.

Quellmalz, E., Shields, P. M., & Knapp, M. S. (1995). *School-based reform: Lessons from a national study. A guide for school reform teams.* Retrieved on September 17, 2002 from http://www.ed.gov/pubs/Reform/pt4.html

Quinn, D. W., Stewart, M., & Nowakowski, J. (1993). An external evaluation of systemwide school reform in Chicago. *International Journal of Educational Reform, 2*(1), 2-11.

Ragland, M. A., Asera, R., & Johnson, J. F. (1999). *Urgency, responsibility, efficacy: Preliminary findings of a study of high-performing Texas school districts.* Austin, TX: University of Texas at Austin, The Charles A. Dana Center.

Raisch, C. D., & Rogus, J. F. (1995). Helping the troubled principal: The central office's formal role in boosting marginal performers. *The School Administrator, 52*(5), 12-15.

Ravitch, D., & Viteritti, J. P. (1997). Introduction. In D. Ravitch & J. Viteritti (Eds.), *New schools for a new century: The redesign of urban education* (pp. 1-16). New Haven, CT: Yale University Press.

Resnick, L. B., & Glennan, T. K. (2001). *Leadership for learning: A theory of action for urban school districts.* Pittsburgh, PA: University of Pittsburgh, HPLC Project, Learning Research and Development Center.

Resnick, L. B., & Harwell, M. (2000, June) *Instructional variation and student achievement in a standards-based education district* (CSE Technical Rep. No. 522). Los Angeles: University of California, Graduate School of Education and Information Studies, National Center for Research on Evaluation, Standards and Student Testing, Center for the Study of Evaluation.

Ross, S. M. (2001). *Creating critical mass for restructuring: What we can learn from Memphis.* (AEL Policy Briefs). Charleston, WV: Appalachia Educational Laboratory.

Rossi, R. J. (2000). *Effective elements: Promoting high achievement in districts and schools serving predominantly low-income middle and high school students.* Washington, DC: American Institutes for Research.

Rowan, B. (1982). Instructional management in historical perspective. *Educational Administration Quarterly, 18*(1), 43-59.

Sanders, W. L. & Rivers, J. C. (1996). *Cumulative and residual effects of teachers on future student academic achievement.* Knoxville, TN: University of Tennessee, Value-Added Research and Assessment Center.

Scambio, E. J., & Graber, J. (1991). Reform through state intervention. *The School Administrator, 48*(7), 8, 10, 12, 14.

Seagren, A. T., & Geering, A. D. (1980, August). *A process to determine professional development needs of principals in a school district.* Paper presented at the annual meeting of the National Conference of Professors of Educational Administration, Norfolk, VA.

Sherman, H., & Jaeger, T. (1995). Professional development: Teachers' communication and collaboration—keys to student achievement. *Mathematics Teaching in the Middle School, 1,* 454-58.

Shipengrover, J., & Conway, J. (1996). *Expecting excellence: Creating order out of chaos in a school district.* Thousand Oaks, CA: Corwin Press.

Simon, E., Foley, E., & Passantino, C. (1998). *Making sense of standards: Implementation issues and the impact on teaching practice. Children achieving: Philadelphia's education reform.* (Progress report series 1996-1997). Philadelphia: University of Pennsylvania, Consortium for Policy Research in Education, Graduate School of Education.

Skrla, L., Scheurich, J. J., & Johnson, J. F. (2000). *Equity-driven achievement-focused school districts.* Austin, TX: University of Texas, The Charles A. Dana Center.

Slavin, R. (1987). A theory of school and classroom organization. *Educational Psychologist, 22*(2), 89-108.

Slavin, R., & Madden, N. (1999). *Disseminating Success for All: Lessons for policy and practice* (Rep. No. 30). Baltimore, MD & Washington, DC: Center for Research on the Education of Students Placed at Risk.

Smith, S. S., & Mickelson, R. A. (2000). All that glitters is not gold: School reform in Charlotte-Mecklenburg. *Educational Evaluation and Policy Analysis, 22*(2), 107-127.

Smylie, M. A., Wenzel, S. A., & Fendt, C. R. (2003). The Chicago Annenberg Challenge: Lessons on leadership for school development. In J. Murphy & A. Datnow (Eds.), *Leadership for school reform: Lessons from comprehensive school reform designs,* (pp. 202-241). Thousand Oaks, CA: Corwin Press.

Snipes, J., Doolittle, F., & Herlihy, C. (2002). *Foundations for success: Case studies of how urban school systems improve student achievement.* Washington, DC: The Council of the Great City Schools.

Snyder, J. (1999). *New Haven Unified School District: A teaching quality system for excellence and equity.* New York: National Commission on Teaching & America's Future.

Spillane, J. P. (2000). *District leaders' perceptions of teacher learning* (CPRE Occasional Paper Series OP-05). Philadelphia: University of Pennsylvania, Consortium for Policy Research in Education, Graduate School of Education.

Spillane, J. P., & Thompson, C. L. (1997). Reconstructing conceptions of local capacity: The local education agency's capacity for ambitious instructional reform. *Educational Evaluation and Policy Analysis, 19*(2), 185-203.

Spiri, M. H. (2001, May). *School leadership and reform: Case studies of Philadelphia principals.* Philadelphia: Consortium for Policy Research in Education.

Sproull, L. S., & Zubrow, D. (1981a). Performance information in school systems: Perspectives from organizational theory. *Educational Administration Quarterly, 17*(3), 61-79.

Sproull, L. S., & Zubrow, D. (1981b). Standardized testing from the administrative perspective. *Phi Delta Kappan, 62*(9), 28-31.

Stecher, B. M., Alkin, M. C., & Flesher, G. (1981). *Patterns of information use in school level decision making* (CSE Rep. No. 160). Los Angeles: University of California, Graduate School of Education and Information Studies, Center for the Study of Evaluation.

Stein, M. K., & D'Amico, L. (1999). *Leading school- and district-wide reform: Multiple subjects matter.* Pittsburgh, PA: University of Pittsburgh, HPLC Project, Learning Research and Development Center.

Stein, M. K., D'Amico, L., & Israel, N. (1998). *Observations, conversations, and negotiations: Administrator support of literacy practices in New York City's Community School District #2.* Pittsburgh, PA: University of Pittsburgh, HPLC Project, Learning Research and Development Center.

Stein, M. K., Harwell, M., & D'Amico, L. (1999). *Toward closing the gap in literacy instruction.* Pittsburgh, PA: University of Pittsburgh, HPLC Project, Learning Research and Development Center.

Steineger, M., & Sherman, L. (2001). Eye of the storm: The central office is the pivotal player in standards-based reform. *Northwest Education* 7(1), 46-51.

Stoll, L., & Fink, D. (1992). Effective school change: The Halton approach. *School Effectiveness and School Improvement, 3*(1), 19-41.

Stringfield, S. (1994). A model of elementary school effects. In D. Reynolds, B. P. M. Creemers, P. S. Nesselrodt, E.C. Schaffer, S. Stringfield, & C. Teddlie (Eds.), *Advances in school effectiveness research and practice* (pp. 153-187). Tarrytown, NY: Pergamon.

Stringfield, S. (1997). Underlying the chaos of factors explaining exemplary U.S. elementary schools: The case for high reliability organizations. In T. Townsend (Ed.), *Restructuring and quality: Problems and possibilities for tomorrow's schools* (pp. 143-160). London: Routledge.

Stringfield, S., Datnow, A., Borman, G., & Rachuba, L. (1999). *National evaluation of core knowledge implementation: Final report.* Baltimore: Center for Social Organization of Schools, Johns Hopkins University.

Stringfield, S., Millsap, M., & Herman, R. (1997). *Special strategies for education disadvantaged children: Results and policy implications.* Washington, DC: U.S. Department of Education.

Sukstorf, M., Wells, A. S., & Crain, R. (1993). A re-examination of Chubb and Moe's Politics, Markets, and America's Schools. In E. Rasell & R. Rothstein (Eds.), *School choice: Examining the evidence* (pp. 209-218). Washington, DC: Economic Policy Institute.

Swaim, S. (1996). The central office role in middle-level school reform. *The School Administrator, 53*(6), 6-9.

Swainston, T. (1982). *Linking testing and evaluation with school district instructional programs.* (ERIC Document Reproduction Service No. ED230626).

Teddlie, C., & Reynolds, D. (2000). *The international handbook of school effectiveness research.* New York: The Falmer Press.

Terry, P. M. (1996, August). *The principal and instructional leadership.* Paper presented at the annual meeting of the National Council of Professors of Educational Administration, Corpus Christi, TX.

Thomas, J. Y. (2002). *The public school superintendency in the 21st century: The quest to define effective leadership* (Rep. No. 55). Baltimore, MD and Washington, DC: Center for Research on the Education of Students Placed at Risk.

Tighe, E., Wang, A., & Foley, E. (2002). *An analysis of the effect of Children Achieving on student achievement in Philadelphia elementary schools.* Philadelphia: Consortium for Policy Research in Education.

Useem, E., & Farley, E. (2004). *Philadelphia's teaching, hiring, and school assignment practices: Comparisons with other districts.* Philadelphia: Research for Action.

Valentine, J. W., & Bowman, M. L. (1988). Audit of principal effectiveness: A method for self-improvement. *NASSP Bulletin, 72*(508), 18-26.

Walter, F. (2002). *District leader's guide to reallocating resources.* Portland, OR: Northwest Regional Educational Laboratory.

Walter, K., & Hassell, B. C. (2000). *Guide to working with model providers.* Retrieved January 7, 2003 from http://www.ncrel.org/csri/gwwmp/

Weathersby, J., & Harkreader, S. (1999, April). *Staff development and student achievement: Making the connection.* Paper presented at the annual meeting of the American Educational Research Association, Montreal, Canada.

Weeres, J. G. (1993). The organizational structure of urban educational systems: Bureaucratic practices in mass societies. In S.W. Rothstein (Ed.), *Handbook of schooling in urban America* (pp. 113-129). Westport, CT: Greenwood Press.

Weick, K. E. (1976). Educational organizations as loosely coupled systems. *Administrative Science Quarterly, 21*(1), 1-19.

Weick, K. E. (1982). Administering education in loosely coupled schools. *Phi Delta Kappan, 63*(10), 673-76.

West, R. F., & Rhoton, C. (1994). School district administrators' perceptions of educational research and barriers to research utilization. *ERS Spectrum, 12*(1), 23-30.

Williams, R. C., & Bank, A. (1982a). *Linking testing and evaluation activities with instruction: Can school districts make it happen?* (CSE Rep. No. 184). Los Angeles: University of California, Graduate School of Education and Information Studies, Center for the Study of Evaluation.

Williams, R. C., & Bank, A. (1982b). *Uses of data to improve instruction in local school districts: Problems and possibilities* (CSE Rep. No. 167). Los Angeles: University of California, Graduate School of Education and Information Studies, Center for the Study of Evaluation.

Williams, R. C., & Bank, A. (1983). *The important district role in educational reform* (CSE Rep. No. 206). Los Angeles: University of California, Graduate School of Education and Information Studies, Center for the Study of Evaluation.

Williams, R. C., & McGranahan, P. (1983). *School district evaluation offices: Are they worth the money?* (CSE Rep. No. 202). Los Angeles: University of California, Graduate School of Education and Information Studies, Center for the Study of Evaluation.

Wilson, B. L. (1985). *School Assessment Survey (SAS) manual: Information for school improvement.* Philadelphia: Research for Better Schools.

Wilson, B. L., & McGrail, J. L. (1987). *Measuring school climate: Questions and considerations.* Philadelphia: Research for Better Schools.

Wimpelberg, R. K. (1987). The dilemma of instructional leadership and a central role for central office. In W. Greenfield (Ed.), *Instructional leadership: Concepts, issues and controversies* (pp. 100-117). Boston: Allyn & Bacon.

Wimpelberg, R. K. (1988). Instructional leadership and ignorance: Guidelines for the new studies of direct administrators. *Education and Urban Society, 20*(3), 302-10.

Wise, A. E., Darling-Hammond, L., & Berry B. (1987). *Effective teacher selection: From recruitment to retention.* Santa Monica, CA: RAND Corporation.

Wong, K. K. (1992). The politics of urban education as a field of study: An interpretive analysis. In J. Cibulka, R. Reed, & K. Wong (Eds.), *Politics of Education Association Yearbook 1991. The Politics of Urban Education in the United States* (pp. 3-26). London: The Falmer Press.

Wong, K. K., Anagnostopoulos, D., Routledge, S., & Edwards, C. (2001). *The challenge of improving instruction in urban high schools: Case studies of the implementation of the Chicago academic standards.* Chicago: Spencer Foundation.

Wood, F. H. (1997). New roles for central office administration in school-based change and staff development. In S.D. Caldwell (Ed.), *Professional development in learning-centered schools* (pp. 64-90). Oxford, OH: National Staff Development Council.

Wraga, W. G. (2002). Recovering curriculum practice: Continuing the conversation. *Educational Researcher, 31*(6), 17-19.

Yap, K., Douglas, I., Railsback, J., Shaughnessy, J., & Speth, T. (2000). *Evaluating whole school reform efforts: A guide for district and school staff* (2nd ed.). Portland, OR: Northwest Regional Educational Laboratory.

Yonezawa, S., & Stringfield, S. (2000). *Special strategies for educating disadvantaged students follow-up study: Examining the sustainability of research-based school reforms.* Baltimore: Johns Hopkins University, CRESPAR.

Index

A

Accelerated Schools—37, 38, 39

accountability data—60

Aspiring Leaders Program—46

C

Center for the Study of Evaluation (CSE)—58, 64

charter schools—66, 79, 80

Children Achieving—19, 21, 33, 47, 48

coaching—38, 46, 53, 55

Coalition of Essential Schools (CES)—39

D

district case studies—9, 18, 26, 67, 68

E

evaluation data—59, 60

F

feedback loops—62, 72

H

human capital—30, 31, 41, 49, 52

S

W

ERS   Subscriptions at a Glance

If you are looking for reliable preK-12 research to . . .

- tackle the challenges of NCLB;

- identify research-based teaching practices;

- make educationally sound and cost-effective decisions; and most importantly

- improve student achievement . . .

then look no further than an ERS Subscription.

Simply pick the subscription option that best meets your needs:

■ **School District Subscription**—a special research and information subscription that provides education leaders with timely research on priority issues in preK-12 education. All new ERS publications and periodicals, access to customized information services through the ERS special library, and 50 percent discounts on additional ERS resources are included in this subscription for one annual fee. This subscription also provides the entire administrative staff "instant" online, searchable access to the wide variety of ERS resources. You'll gain access to the ERS electronic library of more than 1,600 educational research-based documents, as well as additional content uploaded throughout the year.

■ **Individual Subscription**—designed primarily for school administrators, staff, and school board members who want to receive a personal copy of new ERS studies, reports, and/or periodicals published and special discounts on other resources purchased.

■ **Other Education Agency Subscription**—available for state associations, libraries, departments of education, service centers, and other organizations needing access to quality research and information resources and services.

Your ERS Subscription benefits begin as soon as your order is received and continue for 12 months. For more detailed subscription information and pricing, contact ERS toll free at 800-791-9308, by email at ers@ers.org, or visit us online at www.ers.org!

ERS e-Knowledge Portal...
The RIGHT knowledge ... at the RIGHT time ...
in the RIGHT format ... for education leaders!

You can visit us online to locate research, information on what works, and data from vetted sources. The ERS e-Knowledge Portal provides numerous opportunities to find timely and quality resources to assist you in your job. The portal is designed to help you:

- **IDENTIFY** quality materials across the scope of preK-12 education and specifically on issues of critical interest to school district leaders;

- **SEARCH, PREVIEW, and DOWNLOAD** the materials that will help you now;

- **CREATE** customized collections of materials from the portal and your own district-based documents;

- **CONTRIBUTE** descriptions of your successful practices to the portal for use by other school leaders, around the country and throughout the world; and

- **COLLABORATE** with colleagues through discussion forums and communities of practice designed to bring together education leaders.

ERS subscribers receive free or discounted access to materials from ERS. In addition, resources from other sources are available for purchase on a per-use basis.

Visit portal.ers.org today for fast access to the preK-12 resources you need!

ERS ORDER FORM FOR RELATED RESOURCES

Quantity	Item Number	Title	Base Price	ERS Individual Subscriber Discount Price	ERS School District Subscriber Discount Price	Total Price
				Price per Item		
	0497	*ERS Focus On... Professional Development for Instructional Improvement*	$90 for package of 15	$67.50 for package of 15	$45 for package of 15	
Single copy only	5396	*Standards for School Leaders*	$40	$30	$20	
Single copy only	5235	*Success for All*	$40	$30	$20	
	0530	*Supporting School Improvement: Lessons from Districts Successfuly Meeting the Challenge*	$28	$21	$14	
		Shipping and Handling** (Add the greater of $4.50 or 10% of purchase price.)				
		Express Delivery** (Add $20 for second-business-day service.)				
**Please double for international orders.					TOTAL PRICE:	

SATISFACTION GUARANTEED! If you are not satisfied with an ERS resource, return it in its original condition within 30 days of receipt and we will give you a full refund.

Visit us online at www.ers.org for a complete listing of resources!

Method of payment:

☐ Check enclosed (payable to ERS)   ☐ P.O. enclosed (Purchase order #_____)

☐ MasterCard   ☐ VISA   ☐ American Express

Name on Card: _____ Credit Card #:_____

Expiration Date: _____ Signature: _____

Ship to: (please print or type) ☐ Dr.   ☐ Mr.   ☐ Mrs.   ☐ Ms.

Name: _____ Position: _____

School District or Agency: _____ ERS Subscriber ID#: _____

Street Address: _____

City, State, Zip: _____

Telephone: _____ Fax: _____

Email: _____

Return completed order form to:
Educational Research Service • 1001 North Fairfax Street, Suite 500 • Alexandria, VA 22314-1587
Phone: 703-243-2100 • Toll Free Phone: 800-791-9308 • Fax: 703-243-1985 • Toll Free Fax: 800-791-9309
Email: ers@ers.org • Web site: www.ers.org